NAPOLEON HILL'S LIFE LESSONS

Napoleon Hill
& Judith Williamson

A publication of
THE NAPOLEON HILL FOUNDATION

SOUND WISDOM
P.O. Box 310
Shippensburg, PA 17257-0310

For more information on publishing and distribution rights, call 717-530-2122 or e-mail info@soundwisdom.com

Quantity Sales. Special discounts are available on quantity purchases by corporations, associations, and others. For details, contact the Sales Department at Sound Wisdom.

International rights inquiries please contact The Napoleon Hill Foundation at 276-328-6700 or email NapoleonHill@uvawise.edu

Reach us on the Internet: www.soundwisdom.com.

ISBN TP: 978-1-937879-76-1
ISBN Ebook: 978-1-937879-77-8

For Worldwide Distribution, Printed in the U.S.A.

Publisher's Notes: Not all references to economy and conditions have been updated from original writing. We think you'll agree that the messages contained in this book are timeless.

While efforts have been made to verify information contained in this publication, neither the author nor the publisher assumes any responsibility for errors, inaccuracies, or omissions.

While this publication is chock-full of useful, practical information; it is not intended to be legal or accounting advice. All readers are advised to seek competent lawyers and accountants to follow laws and regulations that may apply to specific situations.

The reader of this publication assumes responsibility for the use of the information. The author and publisher assume no responsibility or liability whatsoever on the behalf of the reader of this publication.

2 3 4 5 6 7 8 9 / 21 20 19 18
Weekly quotations written by Napoleon Hill
Text written by Judith A. Williamson
Cover/Jacket designer Eileen Rockwell

Introduction

Judith Williamson, Director of the Napoleon Hill World Learning Center, has written a book that you can read, enjoy, and apply to help you accomplish what you may desire in life.

The author has carefully chosen an applicable quote from Napoleon Hill for each week of the year. Next, the writer has used her extensive knowledge of Napoleon Hill's writings coupled with her experience as a professor on the principles of success to relate to the work of Hill to create a profound message for the reader.

You, the reader, can read, study, and apply the messages on the principles that most appeal to you. But I ask that you not neglect any of the principles because all are necessary if you desire to reach your maximum potential that you received at birth.

Once you have completed the book, go back and read it again and take the suggestions and repeat them until they become a part of your being. The end result of your reading, study, and application will help you reach your desires. But, most importantly, the ultimate result will be not what you receive in the process, but the person that you become while on your journey to success.

Don Green
Executive Director
The Napoleon Hill Foundation

Short Lessons on Life
by Napoleon Hill

A definite purpose is not success, but it is the first step which you must take before you can achieve SUCCESS, and if you refuse or neglect taking it, you will soon find yourself drifting in one of those little boats, riding aimlessly over the sea of life, a victim of winds and the waves of circumstance. Very soon this "drifting" becomes a fixed habit, and habits, whether good or bad, are hard to break up or change.

Lesson 1

Human faults are like garden weeds. They grow without cultivation and soon take the place if they aren't thinned out.
—NAPOLEON HILL

Our life is like a garden. We reap what we sow. Seeds of negativity that are planted in our mental garden ultimately grow into a crop of negative actions that choke our success potential. Like any gardener, we must eliminate the weeds before our garden can produce its best harvest.

REFLECTION
No seed shall perish which the soul hath sown.
—JOHN ADDINGTON SYMONDS

SHORT LESSONS ON LIFE
by Napoleon Hill

If you would plant a suggestion deeply, mix it generously with enthusiasm, for enthusiasm is the fertilizer that will insure its rapid growth.

❧ ❧ ❧

Keep your mind on the things you want and off the things you don't want.

$\mathcal{L}$esson 2

*Everything one needs or desires has a way of
showing up as soon as one is ready for it.
"Ready" doesn't mean "wish."*
—NAPOLEON HILL

Each of us creates the personal outcomes that we manifest in our lives. So, the obvious message for those of us seeking success is to model the outcome that we desire to create. Act as if we already have the trait or characteristic we desire, and it will be so—sooner than later! There is an often heard adage that states: what goes around comes around. It is truer than you think.

REFLECTION
*Whatever this power is, I cannot say. All I know
is that it exists . . . and it becomes available only
when you are in that state of mind in which you
know EXACTLY what you want . . . and are fully
determined not to quit until you get it.*
—ALEXANDER GRAHAM BELL

SHORT LESSONS ON LIFE
by Napoleon Hill

*Any idea, plan, purpose or definite aim
which you persistently submit to your
subconscious mind through the medium of
concentration here described, brings to your
aid the force of infinite intelligence until
eventually practical plans of procedure will
flash into your mind during your period of
concentration.*

Lesson 3

*Pick out some person whom you admire and
imitate him or her as closely as you can. This is
hero-worship, but it improves character.*

—NAPOLEON HILL

Napoleon Hill frequently speaks of his Cabinet of Imaginary
Counselors. This is an expression of his creative imagination
and continues to interest many readers. It also sparks some
concern for the mental health of this great motivational
author. Why is it when people attempt to motivate themselves
by reflecting on the great individuals from the distant or recent
past, others assume that they are rubbing shoulders with the
supernatural? Nonsense!

Great speakers and writers not only gain inspiration from
reading biographies of successful people, but they also gain
insight into their own character. Napoleon Hill was ahead of
his time in recognizing that "what we think about we become."
If we dwell on that which is good, we program our
subconscious minds for the goodness that will ultimately
follow. "Garbage in, garbage out" doesn't only apply to
computers. If we continually feed our subconscious mind
garbage in the form of negative thoughts and images, our
"programming" will then accommodate us by producing those
results in our waking world.

A tomato seed always yields a tomato plant—never a peach
tree. Think about it. The law of the Universe delivers exactly
what we program ourselves for on schedule. Dr. Hill's
imaginary Counselors were his method for making his mind

positive. What is wrong with creating your own board of directors for your life? Members could be teachers from your past, departed friends or relatives you respect, and/or historical people that you choose to admire and emulate. Get yourself programmed for success by putting together a phenomenal board of directors that can meet anytime or anywhere you desire, are free of cost, and have no hidden agenda. Solicit the help and expertise of Dr. Hill's imaginary counselors and always get the very best advice, every time.

REFLECTION
God is the silent partner in all great enterprises.
–ABRAHAM LINCOLN

Lesson 4

If life hands you a lemon, don't complain, but
convert it into lemonade and sell it to those
who are thirsty from griping.

—NAPOLEON HILL

Many people come to study Dr. Hill's Philosophy of Success because they are reeling from a recent adversity or loss and are trying to regain their footing in life. As most of us already know, life can deliver some very hard punches and many times we would rather stay down for the count than stand up and recover. At those times it is always appropriate to remind ourselves just what Dr. Hill had to say on the subject of learning from adversity and defeat. He states: "In every adversity and defeat there is a seed of an equal or equivalent benefit."

Notice that he did not say there would be a full blown blessing or advantage immediately due us equal to the adversity or defeat we experienced. Instead, he challenges us to look for the seed that we need to cultivate and nurture into the benefit that the Universe promises to bestow upon us if we just recognize the oak in the acorn, or in other words, the gift in the adversity!

Dr. Hill's *Science of Success* course helps us uncover those seeds that oftentimes remain hidden and latent in our treasure chest of talents. Think back and remember a few adversities that you may have experienced over the past few years—large or small. Now, honestly ask yourself what "good" came out of the "bad" experience? That seed of good is the compensation that the Universe is "gifting" you so that you can plant it, cultivate it, and harvest it as the reward that has been promised.

<u>REFLECTION</u>

If you have made mistakes . . . there is always another chance for you . . . you may have a fresh start any moment you choose, for this thing we call 'failure' is not the falling down, but the staying down.

–MARY PICKFORD

Lesson 5

*The art of being grateful for the blessings you
already possess is of itself the most profound form
of worship, an incomparable gem of prayer.*
—NAPOLEON HILL

February has always been a month for showing our gratitude to others. We are grateful to the groundhog when he doesn't see his shadow on February 2, we are grateful to our loved ones and thank them with a Valentine on February 14, and we are grateful for our Founding Fathers and celebrate them on Presidents' Day. When you think about it, our lives are overflowing with goodness. Just try counting your blessings one evening as you drift off to sleep. You will be fast asleep before you can finish! You can also try listing the things you are grateful for each day in a journal.

Whether you are grateful for your family, position, health, or personal relationships, it always does a person good to count their blessings. Dr. Hill lists some of the adversities that life has thrown in his path in his writings and then reflects on the good these negatives have brought into his life. Looking for the good within the bad takes a little more time, but the rewards are worth it.

Once you can train yourself to focus on a positive outcome no matter what the circumstances of the moment are, you can maintain and cash in on your positive mental attitude every day in every way! As the saying by Emile Coué states: "Every Day in Every Way I Get Better and Better." Each of us can do this most effectively by being a "good-finder"—even in our worst circumstances. Remember—it's all good!

<u>REFLECTION</u>
The value of all riches, money included, consists in the use one makes of them: not in their possession!

—ANDREW CARNEGIE

Lesson 6

*The best way to get favors is to start
handing out favors.*

—NAPOLEON HILL

Andrew Carnegie's favorite principle is said to have been
Going the Extra Mile. Dr. Hill identifies this principle as one of
the BIG FOUR because of its positive impact on a person's life
and career. By going the extra mile without expectation of
compensation, a person puts even Infinite Intelligence in his
debt. Think about it. Doing just a little extra each day in the
right mental attitude can put you ahead of the masses in just a
short amount of time.

Rendering better service than that which you are paid to
render puts you in a class by yourself because the average
worker simply does not do this.   Essentially, you are
stockpiling up goodness that the law of increasing returns will
reward you with in abundance at some future date. The Laws
of Nature support this, Cosmic Habitforce supports this, and
the Law of Increasing Returns supports this. Emerson's *Essay
on Compensation* discusses this aspect in great detail and is
worth the investment of the time it takes to read it.

By giving more than expected you are paving your road to
greatness. As Emerson states: ". . . do the thing and you shall
have the power." This puts the FORCE squarely in your corner.
If it works, why aren't you using it? Go the extra mile, and
maybe even two, and soon you will understand why this
principle was the one on which Andrew Carnegie based his
entire career.

<u>REFLECTION</u>
If you don't ask, you don't get.

–MAHATMA GANDHI

Lesson 7

*The greatest among men are those who
serve the greatest number.*

—NAPOLEON HILL

In order to adapt ourselves to life's many changes we must first learn to get along with others. Things can't always go our way, benefit us the most, put us in the limelight, or only advance our careers. The "me-first" attitude does not serve a person well for very long. Looking to what we can get rather than to what we can give seems to be a national pastime. I suspect that individuals believe they are holding on to their identity when they refuse to compromise, however, in most of these daily circumstances they are the real losers.

Negotiation takes patience and expertise, and can be elevated to an art form. When done correctly, our long term success depends on it as much as we depend upon water to drink and air to breath. Dr. Hill reminds us multiple times that teamwork is a step on the ladder to success. An even higher step is the formation of a mastermind alliance. In order to reach the summit, you must let go of the desire to be right and autonomous every step of the way.

Being right means little unless you are truly happy. In pursuing success, it is wise to remember that a very real ingredient of success is the ability to get along with and to be liked by others. Without this component any success would be very hollow indeed.

The Universe rewards a giver. When you give without the expectation of return, you create a cycle that revolves around back to you. Ultimately, you are the recipient of the good you put out there. Start a ripple of giving right now, and watch out for the wave of goodness you will have soon created! Remember "what goes around comes around." Make what comes around to you only good by starting the ripple that creates the wave!

<u>**REFLECTION**</u>
My best friend is the one who brings
out the best in me.

–HENRY FORD

Lesson 8

Fortunate indeed is the man who has learned to put the spirit of play into his daily work. He will live longer and earn more.

—NAPOLEON HILL

Laughter may truly be the best medicine. Norman Cousins speaks about it in *An Anatomy of an Illness* and Napoleon Hill speaks about it frequently. Laughter can be our personal armor against negativity and the harshness the world brings to bear on us. Why start your day with the woes of the world by reading the morning newspaper or watching the news? Why not begin each morning with a hearty portion of laughter and lightheartedness? Choosing one over the other can make the difference in how your day develops.

Great thinkers of the world all affirm that we control our thoughts, our repeated thoughts mold our character, and our character creates our destiny. Wholesome laughter, like good food for our body, nourishes our character in many ways. Thoughts are things both literally and metaphorically. You've heard the saying, "You are what you eat." Likewise, what you think about you become. Thinking good thoughts creates good endorphins in your physical body, and causes you to reap the just rewards of a healthier and happier you!

It's not necessary to be life's victim. Become the VICTOR by learning how to address many of the worst experiences life can dish out to you. Respond with laughter, and say what W. Clement Stone, Napoleon Hill's partner for over a decade, said no matter what happened—"That's good." And, remember it's always good. There is no other alternative for the person with a positive mental attitude.

<u>REFLECTION</u>
Cheerfulness and contentment are great beautifiers and are famous preservers of good looks.
–CHARLES DICKENS

Lesson 9

*An educated man is one who has learned how
to get what he wants without violating the
rights of other.*

—NAPOLEON HILL

The essay entitled *Tolerance* by Dr. Napoleon Hill is one of the most requested of his short works. I remember just after 9/11, a woman phoned in from New York wanting permission to copy this short piece and place it under office doors in the city. Her idea was to remind people that before hasty conclusions were reached, one should pause and think. This is good advice at any time, not just in situations when we are in our fight or flight mode.

Tolerance like patience comes hard for many people. Culturally, individuals may view their way of doing things the "correct" way because that is how they were brought up, but education supplies us with equally "correct" alternative ways of thinking.   For example, when carrying a bouquet of flowers in the United States, the bouquet is held upright—flowers positioned with the blooms on top. However, in Japan flowers are carried in the opposite manner—blooms facing down—because it is believed that the life force of the flowers will not run out as quickly if carried this way, and the recipient of the bouquet will have longer to enjoy the blooms! Which way is correct? One or the other, or both?

People tend to be intolerant of things they do not understand. For them, difference often equates to being wrong. Whereas, if time were spent in learning about the culture and the customs of others, perhaps alternative ways of seeing things would open up. Years ago when I was preparing a Mexican meal at home for my father, I opened up a can of refried beans. My dad asked me what they were, and when I told him that they were refried beans, he commented—speaking from his German background—that now he had seen everything. "I can't believe it," he stated, "now they are canning leftovers!" As you can see, his awareness of Mexican cuisine was limited.

Tolerance is something worth cultivating. Just as we cultivate a taste for fine wine and good food, we must work up to a higher understanding of people, their customs, activities, and cultural nuances. Misunderstandings, strife, and petty annoyances are all too common during our time here on earth. Why not, as Dr. Hill suggests, cross over into living a more tolerant life that focuses on what our commonalities are rather than our differences? This heightened understanding does not mean we "cross over" to the other side's way of doing something. Rather, it means that we understand their meaning behind the action. This understanding is one step closer to living in harmony rather than discord. See if, just for today, you can step aside and place yourself in another's shoes. Work to see it from their perspective before you critique something they have done. Afterward, consider your conditioned response anew. Maybe, just maybe, you might see something intolerable from a different perspective. Then you will be a step in the right direction toward making our world a better place in which to live by dealing with one intolerable thing at a time.

REFLECTION
*I'm always ready to learn, although I do not
always like being taught.*
–WINSTON CHURCHILL

*L*esson 10

Examine most carefully the things
you desire most.

−NAPOLEON HILL

What would it feel like to be the richest man in the world? Ask yourself that question with a notepad in front of you and a pen in hand. Now, write down a listing of what you would experience if finances were readily available. Remember, to consider first what makes you happy now because your interests, values, and beliefs probably will not change much even if you acquire money. Do you enjoy the outdoors, an elegant dinner out, chats with the neighbors, a good book and a good movie, a comfortable house and labor saving appliances, a loyal pet, and children who respect you?

Notice as you write your list which ones are contingent on having finances, and which ones are brought about directly by your state of mind. Funny, but it has been said that our attitude creates our altitude. This could be reversed as well: the higher we look up, the more positive our attitude. Interesting. Hummm. Instead of complaining about the worn shoes on our feet, reflect on how an amputee feels. Instead of bemoaning the job we work at daily, talk to a person out of work. Instead of turning up your nose at last night's leftovers, volunteer in a soup kitchen. Instead of reciting a litany of woes about the behavior of your children, talk to a person who has lost a child.

You see, riches are inside each and every one of us if we know where to look for our bounty. By locating and treasuring what you love about each and every day of your life, you will increase your personal net worth held in your Success account. It's not the value in your checkbook, but the value in your heart that make you the richest man in the world! Start your savings account now by listing what exactly it is that makes you rich beyond measure. Therein you will find your greatest treasure and it is pure gold indeed.

<u>REFLECTION</u>
First say to yourself what you would be; and then do what you have to do.

–EPICTETUS

Lesson 11

Spoken words leave impressions.   Printed words leave tracks.
—NAPOLEON HILL

Napoleon Hill's *Code of Ethics* is essentially his instructional manual for life. Early on in years, he outlined what he felt to be his rationale for living a good and productive lifestyle. These 11 points became his commandments for living optimally. Many of us voice our beliefs about what we should and shouldn't do, but seldom do we write these points down.

Unwritten beliefs are quickly overlooked and not followed. People can easily say they have forgotten what their focus was, and thereby failed to remember what they were supposed to do. The old adage "out of sight, out of mind" rings true here. However, when something is written down, it serves as a contract between yourself and the written page. When you literally face it and read it, you are obliged to acknowledge your own words because they are staring back at you. You are less likely to weasel out of living up to your best expectations of yourself.

As Napoleon Hill knew, if you honor your word you are honoring yourself. Why not create your own code of ethics today?   Read it through once in the morning, once in the afternoon, and once just before retiring. Ask yourself, "Am I walking my talk?"   If not, you need to reevaluate your commitment to living a truly healthy, happy, and terrific life.

REFLECTION
A drop of ink may make a million think.
—LORD BYRON

SHORT LESSONS ON LIFE
by Napoleon Hill

Until you have learned to be tolerant with those who do not always agree with you—until you have cultivated the habit of saying some kind word of those whom you do not admire—until you have formed the habit of looking for the good instead of the bad there is in others, you will be neither successful nor happy.

An acorn never produces a pine nor does a pine cone ever produce an oak, and nothing is ever produced that does not have its antecedents in something else which preceded it.

Lesson 12

You are where you are because of your habits of thought.
—NAPOLEON HILL

Dr. Hill's *Creed for Riches* is a powerful statement that reads almost like one long affirmation. Stating his beliefs in the present tense ensures that his riches are in the here and now instead of the distant future. Indicating his gratitude for the riches received endears him to the Universe as well because he is not bemoaning a loss, but rather giving thanks for all the goodness that the Universe has bestowed upon him.

Dr. Hill knew that an attitude of gratitude will carry a person farther than complaining will. Just observe for yourself how far a complaint will carry you in today's world versus a sincere compliment. Compliments create thankfulness while complaints create unrest. People who complain are people to be dealt with and are often not invited to social gatherings. People who compliment are sought after and are fun to be around. Aggressive, belligerent, hostile people seldom align themselves with others. However, people who look for the good while oftentimes overlooking the bad are people others seek out.

Positive reinforcement is good for the soul and good for our neighbors simultaneously. Work at being a good-finder rather than a fault-finder. If you make it a habit, your world will improve tremendously.

REFLECTION:
You are the sum total of all the causes and effects you have set up in yourself through your mental and emotional attitudes. Their end result is the you that you are right this minute!
—CLAUDE M. BRISTOL

SHORT LESSONS ON LIFE
by Napoleon Hill

Here is a formula that has helped many to change their world: What the mind can conceive and believe the mind can achieve. Have you memorized this formula?

❧ ❧ ❧

Men who sow the seed of dissention always expect to reap a crop of something they didn't earn.

Lesson 13

Do it now . . . and before
anyone tells you to do it!
—NAPOLEON HILL

The one outstanding character trait that parents can instill in their children is self-confidence. If you possess self-confidence, many things naturally work in your favor. Believing in yourself and your ability to succeed at whatever you put your mind to is a priceless asset that cannot be purchased at any cost. Knowing that you have an innate "can-do" attitude prevents you from accepting failure as either part of your genetic makeup or your destiny.

Instilling confidence in others is no easy task, let alone calling it up from the depths of your own being when you have a need for it yourself. Self-confidence often eludes us when we need it the most. Feelings of insecurity, ineptitude, or simple inadequacy cause us to feel as if everyone else possesses more of the success making ingredients than we do. These feelings, if addressed at the onset, can be circumvented through action.

Dr. Hill recommends repetition of positive affirmations until the affirmations become second nature. Once these affirmations become habitual and strongly rooted in our subconscious minds, we can call on them at will to strengthen us and to protect us against anything that may sap our self-confidence. Many times by just recalling a time in your past wherein you were exemplary in your approach to an issue or acted in a powerful way, you can call up that very same emotional feeling and relive it in order to produce another positive outcome.

To paraphrase Emerson, by doing the thing we want to accomplish we cultivate the power to do it. "Do the thing and you shall have the power," is Emerson's wording. This is a strong, positive statement, and one that we can take to the bank. If we want to be strongly self-confident, we must place our personal power in the self-confidence we already possess and use it wisely. To have self-confidence, be self-confident. Practice makes perfect! Dr. Hill reminds us that actions are first cobwebs, and then cables. Why not begin now by building your self-confidence level? Then when you need it the most, you will already have it in place to work for you at a moment's notice. Remember W. Clement Stone's command, "Do it now!"

REFLECTION
How wonderful it is that nobody need
wait a single moment before starting to
improve the world.   –ANNE FRANK

Lesson 14

*Sometimes it is wiser to join forces with
an opponent than it is to fight.*
—NAPOLEON HILL

One of the hardest things anyone must do in life is to forgive others who have wronged or harmed them. Forgiving is one of the initial steps in maintaining a positive mental attitude. Hatred and anger can be defined as two-edged swords that not only hurt the victim, but hurt the perpetrator as well. Sometimes it feels good to nurse our anger and to allow ourselves some righteous indignation. This may feel like a powerful choice in the beginning, but it quickly can spiral down into self-pity. Hatred and anger are enemies to our healing. At times we tell ourselves that our anger is justified and needs to be acted upon in a negative way, i.e., an eye for an eye mentality. Why this may be partially true for initial healing, it is equally true that people who harbor hate and discontent can destroy themselves from the inside out due to their lethal concentration of emotion.

Some people are spurred to action because of their anger, and this can be either good or bad as well. If anger motivates an individual to do something positive, then the outcome can be healing. However, if anger motivates an individual to do something negative, we all know that two wrongs do not make a right. Getting ourselves to decide the best course of action for our positive outcome and then acting on that plan takes courage and self-confidence. It is easier to wallow in self-pity and blame another for the life you are leading, but it proves only one thing—that you choose not to be accountable for the end result. If you give way to hatred and allow it to fester deep within your most intimate self, you will only clog your soul's arteries that lead to your higher self and ultimately your highest good. Why let someone rob you of your bliss? Take control, take action, and blow the smoke of the past away so that you can clearly see the horizon. Forgive to benefit the most important person in your world—you!

REFLECTION
We build too many walls and not enough bridges.

–SIR ISAAC NEWTON

Lesson 15

You have the power to create anything you can imagine! Act on the ideas produced by your imagination . . . you will achieve success.

—NAPOLEON HILL

Napoleon Hill discusses the permanence of change as the only certainty we have in life. And, he elaborates upon the idea that we must use what we have or lose it. These two concepts go back to what Dr. Hill states are the only two things the Universe will not tolerate. One is inactivity and the other is a vacuum.

In order to create movement toward success one must be action oriented. Without action, nothing moves. Thoughts definitely are things that create the momentum for movement, but action must always follow thought in order to bring about results.

Vacuums are areas of emptiness that attract whatever claims the available space first. Ask yourself if you can ever have an empty table in your home without something soon filling it? Newspapers, bills, mailings, purchases, dishes, etc., all congregate in open spaces. The message Napoleon Hill has for us who deal with this dilemma is fill the void in your own life first before someone or something fills it for you!

In our lives we have open spaces waiting to be filled. These can exist in opportunities that we have not taken or have decided not to act on. The situations wherein we prefer not to act can soon add up and create many holes or voids in our lives. So you have decided not to have a definite major purpose, no problem! Your boss will find something for you to do that will fill that void. It might not be your purpose, but guess what? Now your time has been taken and the vacuum filled by something you would rather not be doing in the first place. Your open space was grabbed by someone else, and the vacuum was filled!

Voids exist in our lives—if we allow them to exist—in the following areas: mental, physical, social, spiritual, and emotional. Unfortunately, by ignoring something it seldom goes away. Usually it gets bigger and uglier and soon becomes a mess for us to clean up. Vacuums filled by the Universe are usually not bearing gifts of success, but another disadvantage we have to overcome.

Dr. Hill states that if these are universal laws, we should acknowledge them and deal with them directly. This means that we should be active and purposeful in the major areas of our lives. Also, when we sense something is missing, it probably is. Are you missing relationships, exercise, love, education, or a sense of the divine? Then decide for yourself how you want to fill this void in your life. If you relax and wait for the vacuum to be filled, it will, but not in the way you might have chosen. Be active, be purposeful, and be directed. Chart your course based on the very best future you envision for yourself. Nobody can do it for you. Your inner light or "starlight" shines for you first. Acquire it and then pass it on as your personal gift to the Universe.

REFLECTION
The world is but a canvas to the imagination.
–HENRY DAVID THOREAU

Lesson 16

*Your progress in life begins in your own mind
and ends in the same place.*

—NAPOLEON HILL

It's never too late to begin again! As long as you are breathing, you can make a new start. Make a commitment to begin something new today. All too often we focus on missed opportunities and past mistakes that we allow to hold us back. However, when we close those doors and begin to consider fresh, new ideas that we can be enthusiastic about, we always find success playing hide-and-seek right behind the door we just opened.

Isn't it amazing that when we make a clean sweep of things, newborn ideas just pour into our minds? Spring is a time for spring cleaning. This does not just apply to your home or office, but to your mental attitude as well. Take inventory of your old musty ideas, past practices, and lost causes. Consider throwing them away. These old ideas may be the ghosts of ideas long past that still live in your subconscious mind. They need to be put to rest for good. Now, we may also have some old dust bunnies that are lurking just below our daily thoughts and duties that need to be swept away too. Do it now! Get rid of the old and bring in the new. Consider what you might have been if your dreams had come true. Rather than wasting more time lamenting what might have been, begin to make it so today. Grandma Moses wasn't too old to become an artist in her old age, and neither are you. Don't become a "has-been" before you are somebody. You have the "know how" if you just do it now.

Live your life's dream before somebody else does. Only you can do it, and the fact is that you are not getting any younger. Today is the day. The time is now. You are the best person for the job. Do it now, and you will thank yourself for the rest of your life. As we have heard before, it is not too late to become the person that you might have been! Be somebody!

REFLECTION
A man cannot directly choose his circumstances,
but he can choose his thoughts, and so indirectly,
yet surely, shape his circumstances.

–JAMES ALLEN

Lesson 17

Close the door of fear behind you, and see how
quickly the door to success opens in front of you.
—NAPOLEON HILL

Are you an armchair traveler? Do you daydream or read about places that you would like to visit at a future date? Maybe you even send off for travel brochures or surf the net in order to find the best deals on land excursions or cruises. Possibly you even inquire about courses that you can study abroad. Gathering information is good, but going is better! Do not mistake the acquisition of knowledge that you gather through research and study as the real journey. At best it is a virtual trip. As a prerequisite, there is nothing wrong with planning. It is essential, but don't stop there.

Napoleon Hill gives us his blueprint for success in his marvelous book, ***Think and Grow Rich.*** Literally, it appears on every page if we are ready to receive it. The "secret" is only hidden from those who are not astute enough to discover the message that is read both on the page and between the lines.

In Hill's article "Road Map To Success," Dr. Hill gives us the recipe for creating a map for our own success journey. Why not give it a try? Why not sit down with a journal and pen in hand, and outline your journey? Next, reread your specific directions several times per day, and then take the very first step in actualizing your dreams. No vision—no destination. See it and create!

Many people say that life does not come with an instruction manual! They are correct. We did not receive one at birth. But, to make up for that deficiency, Dr. Hill has created the success manual for the rest of our life—from this moment on— and it's available to you right now. Make certain that you read the book, *Think and Grow Rich*, if you want to create the life that you have only been dreaming about! It is the instruction manual of choice the world over. "Whatever the mind can conceive and believe, the mind can achieve," states Dr. Hill. Here are the ABCs of success, but only backward. Conceive, Believe, Achieve! Read the book that discloses the real secret to a happy and successful life. Do it now!

REFLECTION
We must travel in the direction of our fear.
-JOHN BERRYMAN

Lesson 18

*The seven basic fears include the fear of poverty,
criticism, ill health, loss of love, old age, loss of
liberty, death. Since fear is merely a state of mind,
you can control it by taking action.*

—NAPOLEON HILL

You probably have heard that fear is faith in reverse. If you are
fearful, you are not faithful. On the other hand, courage has
been said to be fear that has said its prayers. You get the idea.
When you feel fear and it impedes your progress you are
becoming a "Doubting Thomas." Stuck in your tracks, you
cannot move forward because your feet are glued to the
ground by fear. No one likes this feeling when we experience
it, but nearly all of us have felt the emotion of fear and for a
period of time allowed it to stall our actions. Fear can stop us
dead in our tracks toward success.

Napoleon Hill is said to have coined the phrase "We have
nothing to fear but fear itself." This became FDR's call to arms
during the great depression. The President challenged the
country to overcome the fear of poverty that was holding it
back. Poverty is a state of mind and can be eradicated. At this
time, the nation had to be reminded of this in order to advance.
Dr. Hill wrote **Think and Grow Rich** in 1937 just when our
country needed it the most. Victory gardens, fireside chats,
and **Think and Grow Rich** were the prescription given to a
country struggling to overcome the Great Depression.

Dr. Joe Dudley of Dudley Products, Inc. is an outstanding
example of a person who has overcome his personal fears for

the betterment of thousands of people globally. He tells the story of beginning his business in his kitchen sink where he made hair care products by night so that he could sell them by day. Today, a little over 40 years later he is a millionaire many times over who gives back to his community, his employees, and his family. This success came about because of Dr. Hill's directive in the final chapter of *Think and Grow Rich* to overcome the Ghosts of Fear!

Dr. Dudley attributes his success to *Think and Grow Rich.* He states that he has read this book over 300 times. He challenges himself, his staff, his family, and anyone desiring riches to spend six hours one day per week studying this book. He states without reservation that this is what has made him the success that he is today. By studying the chapters so intently, Dr. Dudley explains that you open up your subconscious mind during hours three and four, and then during hours five and six you are able to contact the Universal Subconscious Mind. During hours one and two, you set the stage for learning by calming your mind and preparing yourself seriously for the study you are about to undertake. This is a small price to pay for becoming the very top of your field in just four short decades!

When asked if he ever was fearful during his journey to success, Dr. Dudley responded that he still experiences the emotion of fear today. But, he now has the antidote to fear and for him it is being faithful to his extended study and reading of *Think and Grow Rich.* He states that fear can become a cycle and whenever a person senses that he is about to become fearful about something, right then and there he needs to begin to study the antidote *Think and Grow Rich* and read the book with the explicit intention of finding a solution to whatever problem is causing the fear. For Dr. Dudley, this works every time. When faith enters the picture, fear retreats and the best solution for any problem can always be found!

<u>REFLECTION</u>

Fear is one of the strongest feelings influencing desire, and acts usually as a neutralizer of other feelings and desires, and is most potent as a motive influencing choice or decision—in fact, one is justified in regarding fear as the negative form of desire, being really a "desire-not-to."

—WILLIAM WALTER ATKINSON

SHORT LESSONS ON LIFE
by Napoleon Hill

When that picture grows, or has been forced
to the proportions of an obsession, it is
taken over by the subconscious mind,
through some hidden law of nature which
the wisest of men do not understand. From
that point on one is drawn, attracted or
guided in the direction of the physical
equivalent of the mental picture.

Lesson 19

Your ship will not come in unless you have first sent one out. A Positive Mental Attitude (PMA) is the right mental attitude. It determines whether you act favorably or unfavorably, constructively or destructively, positively or negatively. A person with PMA aims for high goals and constantly strives to achieve them.

—NAPOLEON HILL

Napoleon Hill has said that when you are ready to receive something it comes to you easily and in abundance. But, he reminds us continually that we must be ready to receive it! If we have not prepared the fertile soil of our subconscious mind to receive what we want to attract, nothing will grow into manifestation. Thoughts will wither and die on the vine because they have not been nurtured and cultivated into the blossoms that represent abundance in whatever form we desire. When you think of the gardening metaphor it is easy to understand why our actions must be timed in order to produce the best results.

Uncultivated gardens produce crops of weeds and debris, not fruits and vegetables. Simply planting seeds without the weeding and tilling that must accompany a good yield, will do little. Gardens take work and so do goals. Little can be expected if we work sporadically at our gardening. Likewise, little progress toward our purpose can be expected unless we devote time and energy toward its nourishment. Keeping our purpose ever present in our mind through daily actions is like weeding, tilling, watering, and feeding our garden. Most often, if these steps are followed regularly, we will be rewarded with a good crop of whatever it is we have planted. Tomato seeds produce tomatoes. Pumpkin seeds produce pumpkins. Like produces like.

Thoughts are things. The thoughts we entertain produce their counterpart in our lives. Angry thoughts produce angry outcomes. Happy thoughts yield happy results. Being aware of this universal law assists us in the proper timing of our results. Seeds planted randomly often do not germinate and grow. But, seeds planted in the proper growing season flourish and bear fruit on schedule. Recognizing that thoughts are like seeds may help us not only to expect a bountiful harvest, but to consider the timing of our planting. Farmers consult the Farmers' Almanac and we can consult *Think & Grow Rich*. It's a good time to plant your garden now!

Napoleon Hill often quoted from the poems of Ella Wheeler Wilcox. Below is a poem that relates to this week's topic.

YOU NEVER CAN TELL
by Ella Wheeler Wilcox

You never can tell when you send a word,
Like an arrow shot from a bow
By an archer blind, be it cruel or kind,
Just where it may chance to go,

It may pierce the breast of your dearest friend,
Tipped with its poison or balm,
To a stranger's heart in life's great mart,
It may carry its pain or its calm.

You never can tell when you do an act
Just what the result will be;
But with every deed you are sowing a seed,
Though the harvest you may not see.

Each kindly act is an acorn dropped
In God's productive soil.
You may not know, but the tree shall grow,
With shelter for those who toil.

You never can tell what your thoughts will do,
In bringing you hate or love;
For thoughts are things, and their airy wings
Are swifter than carrier doves.

They follow the law of the universe,
Each thing must create its kind;
And they speed o'er the track to bring you back
Whatever went out from your mind.

<u>REFLECTION</u>

The man without a purpose is like a ship without a rudder—a waif, a nothing, a no man. Have a purpose in life, and, having it, throw such strength of mind and muscle into your works as God has given you.

–THOMAS CARLYLE

SHORT LESSONS ON LIFE
by Napoleon Hill

*We are where we are and what we are
because of the habits of which we have
become the victims, voluntarily or
involuntarily. We are victims of the habits
of thought and the habits of action. We can
change our station in life—and this is the
only way we can change it—by changing
our habits.*

∿ ∿ ∿

*As I have stated before, the brain is
something like a rich garden spot in that it
will voluntarily grow a fine crop of weeds if
it is not organized and kept busy growing a
more desirable crop.*

Lesson 20

Man is master of his fate because he is master of his attitude. No more effort is required to aim high in life, to demand abundance and prosperity, than is required to accept misery and poverty.

—NAPOLEON HILL

Sometimes short to-the-point declarations make more sense than 500 word essays. Napoleon Hill was fond of these types of sayings and wrote many of them throughout his lifetime. When he began marketing his home study course, he included many of these sayings directly in the course materials and called them Success Vitamins. Hill figured that if we could take daily vitamins for our physical well-being, then we could also ingest success vitamins that would improve our mental health.

Think about it. Doesn't it make perfect sense? What we feed our mind results in who we become. Thoughts do create our destiny over time. If we want positive outcomes, we must think positive thoughts. You don't get tomatoes from pumpkin seeds. Likewise, we get positive results from positive thoughts when you "plant" those thoughts in the garden of your mind. Affirmations and declarations help set our mental course for success. When we repeat these positive ideas, we reinforce positive outcomes. Practice can and does make perfect.

Why not try creating some statements of a positive nature for yourself? You can write these down on 3x5 index cards and repeat them several times a day. These statements should be written in the present tense, have no negative words, be short, and always focused on a positive outcome. Years ago these types of declarations were called "treatments." They were intended as a prescription for concerns of a mental nature. If, for example, a person was a procrastinator, the treatment for this individual might be: "I take charge of my thoughts, feelings, and actions at all times." Another treatment for the same person might be: "I consistently think and act in the direction of my goals and my immediate best outcome."

Inspire and motive yourself by creating 10 personal affirmations for your "higher good" that you recite out loud morning, noon, and night. Say them with emotional intensity too as if the affirmation was already true in this present moment. Your affirmations can become the very vehicle that will transport you to the success destination you want in your life. Remember: "I accomplish all I set my mind on today for my personal good." Just tell yourself that it is truth in advance.

REFLECTION
There are two kinds of discontent in this world:
the discontent that works, and the discontent that
wrings its hands. The first gets what it wants,
and the second loses what it had. There is no cure
for the first but success, and there is no cure at all
for the second.

–ELBERT HUBBARD

Lesson 21

There is a material advantage in being agreeable to other people. You will never be as happy in any other way as you will be when you know that you are making others happy.

—NAPOLEON HILL

The military maxim "Leader of one, leader of many, if you can't lead one, you can't lead any!" contains much truth. Being a true leader requires character paired with a moral conscience. If you are unable to lead yourself first, you cannot direct subordinates. A model leader not only details what is expected, but exemplifies it himself. Many of us have heard the saying, "Do as I say, not as I do." This directive commands no respect because it does not ring true. Any old windbag can "command" respect, but those who truly receive it do not have to command anything. People earn respect based on their actions. They are leaders in their own right because they radiate self-esteem and self-confidence because of the choices they have made and the actions they have taken. No one has to tell them what to do. They instinctively know the path to take.

Today's leader is unlike a military commander. People respond more to a person in charge who appreciates and recognizes them for their valuable contribution to the organization. Many ineffective leaders parrot remarks of recognition, but without sincerity these remarks are perceived by the employees to be worthless platitudes. People know when praise is sincere and heartfelt. Without the accompanying follow-up, praise without commitment to the employees is meaningless.

If you desire to be a leader, the first leadership commandment is Biblical. "Do unto others as you would have others do unto you!" Using people as stepping stones, treating them as second class citizens, undercutting their abilities, and persistently finding fault all create a downward spiral of dissatisfaction. Eventually, the leader will see that he has a regiment of one—himself—and question what went wrong. If he is truthful, he will discover that the only person he considers to have leadership potential is himself. Amazing as this may seem, when a leader of this nature is gone, another does take his or her place. If you are the replacement, think before you act, listen more than you speak, and remember a true leader is recognized for qualities that are people oriented not self-centered. People do perceive the difference. Don't be naive and believe that you have concealed your true colors. Dr. Hill states that ". . . the leader is not recognized so much by what he does himself as by what he inspires others to do."

Be an inspiration to those you lead. Permit them to grow in your presence. Encourage them to be risk-takers. Some will fail and some will succeed. But, every one of them will credit you for having faith in their personal ability to reach for their highest dreams. True leaders inspire others to be the best person they are capable of becoming. When you are this type of leader, you will always have your followers watching your back because you watched theirs!

REFLECTION
The worst sin toward our fellow creatures is not to hate them but to be indifferent to them; that's the essence of inhumanity.
                                    –GEORGE BERNARD SHAW

Lesson 22

*Every word you speak advertises your wisdom or
ignorance. Remember this before speaking.
Communication is the basis for getting along with others.
There is power in the spoken word . . . avoid all-inclusive,
restrictive words such as never, only, nothing, every,
everyone, no one and can't. These should be eliminated
unless you're absolutely certain that they're correct.*

—NAPOLEON HILL

Dr. Hill states that "every adversity carries with it the seed of an equal or greater benefit." This is very apparent in raising children as any parent can readily tell you. Just when you think things can get no worse, you are surprised with some good news that turns things topsy-turvy. Apparently, this is one of those laws of the universe that both Dr. Hill and W. Clement Stone researched. Stone himself was very interested in cycles or the cyclical nature of things. Both Dr. Hill and W. Clement Stone were parents who prided themselves on their children's accomplishments. Both experienced the usual ups and downs of parenthood. But, with certainty, each of them modeled the philosophy of success for their children as only they could.

If you have read Dr. Hill's biography *Lifetime of Riches*, you will surely remember the story about Blair being born with no ears! The doctor who delivered Blair told the Hills that he would never hear in a normal fashion. Dr. Hill would not accept that diagnosis and repeatedly stated that Blair would have normal hearing. He then undertook a method of treatment that allowed Blair to have nearly normal hearing by the time he graduated from college. This is a miracle in itself and is included as a positive testimony as to what the *Science of Success* can do for anyone willing to hold a positive mental attitude and to take action on it. Dr. Hill held a picture of his son Blair as a hearing child in his mind's eye. Eventually, he was able to make this a reality in the here and now. His vision of Blair hearing normally was a consequence of looking for the seed of an equal or greater benefit in Blair's apparent birth defect—his adversity. Blair benefited because of his father's persistent action in making his vision a reality.

Fathers are a good indicator of their children's future success. We've all heard the saying that "The apple does not fall far from the tree." Being blessed with a father who not only challenges his children to succeed is one thing, but having the added advantage of a father who "walks the talk" is another. Stone and Hill shared their vision of success with the world. All of us who read their books are beneficiaries of their beliefs and experiences. When giving thanks, let's remember to give thanks to Dr. Hill and W. Clement Stone for caring enough to bring their self-help motivational philosophy to light for those of us who follow in their footsteps. In many ways, they are our motivational fathers who have charted the course for many of our lives.

Let's toast the two inspirational Fathers of Motivational Literature right now:
   "In the dark and stormy future when storms around you crash, may your heart be full of sunshine and your pockets full of cash."
Seems like a toast both of these fathers would endorse!

REFLECTION
Man's word is his wand filled with magic and power!
—FLORENCE SCOVEL SHINN

Lesson 23

*The successful person is open-minded and tolerant on
all subjects. If you close your mind, you will be shut
off from the recognition of favorable opportunities
and the friendly cooperation of others.*

—NAPOLEON HILL

How many people have you heard exclaim "I love change!"? I
would be willing to bet not too many. Change makes people not
only want to look the other way, but to run the other way! Part
of the problem in accepting change is that many people do not
view it as a process, but as an either-or situation. Nobody likes
to be pressured into making changes that they feel are thrust
upon them. A command that says "Change or else!" seldom
makes a person eager to switch. When viewed as a process,
however, change can be made to feel more palatable.

In teaching *Learning from Adversity and Defeat (Principle # 13)* in
the **Science of Success Course,** I am aware of the difficulty
students experience when dealing with change. My dilemma as
an instructor is how to present the material relevant to change
as a process that can be monitored versus something that an
individual has no control over.

Having read Elisabeth Kublër-Ross' work entitled **On Death
and Dying,** I noticed a similarity between the change process
and the grief/dying process. Dr. Kublër-Ross breaks the
process down into these five stages: denial, anger, bargaining,
depression, and acceptance. When you consider what it is like
to change a habit or something structured in our life, the
process is identical.

For example, if you are told that you smoke too much by your physician and that you need to stop, your interior dialog might go something like this:

1. Denial: *"This can't be happening to me. I am in control of my habits, my habits don't control me!"*
2. Anger: *"How dare my Doctor have the nerve to say this to me? Who is he to tell me how to live my life!"*
3. Bargaining: *"Maybe I could just cut down to a pack of cigarettes a day and that will make me less at risk."*
4. Depression: *"I'm so depressed? I know he is right because of my persistent cough that won't quit! I need help."*
5. Acceptance: *"I know I need help to quit, and my Doctor can help me with quitting. I will take his advice and begin his program."*

Note that this dialog can last a day, week, month, or even longer depending upon how strong your resistance is. The good news is, however, that when you have advanced to the depression stage of the change process you are almost there! You only need to step up to "acceptance" and you will have made the change to a better you. In the above case, a healthier you too.

Now, if you are going through some change in your life, pinpoint where you are by analyzing your interior dialog—how you talk to yourself. Next, note what stage you are in and even if you are not at stage 5, congratulate yourself for knowing that change is a process. Know that you can track your progress as you advance through the stages. The use of knowledge is power, and you have the power to make the change that may have seemed insurmountable before now.

REFLECTION
Great minds have purposes, others have wishes.
Little minds are tamed and subdued by
misfortune; but great minds rise above them.
–WASHINGTON IRVING

Lesson 24

The person who plans his day in advance goes about his work logically and efficiently. When there is no organization of schedule, there is no place to begin.

—NAPOLEON HILL

We have all been told to hitch our wagon to a star, shoot for the moon, reach for the gold, and strive for an A++++ as little Ralphie daydreams about in the holiday movie *A Christmas Story* by Jean Shepherd. When Bing Crosby asks "Would you like to swing on a star, carry moonbeams home in a jar, and be better off than you are?" we all respond with a resounding YES! Granted, it's not hard to wish for success, but how do we make it happen?

Authors specializing in self-help tell us that in order to manifest our dreams, we must have objectives that are observable and measurable. What that means is we must be able to see and to count our actions taken toward achieving our goals and document them. Sounds easy, right?

Well, life often happens and we get busy doing other things and our goals sit on the perimeter of life when they should really be life's bull's eye. How do we realign our arrows in order to hit the small target in the center? Napoleon Hill gives us tips that we can follow. If we remember that we can reach an emotionalized target quicker and more often, we will use our positive emotions to help motivate us to reach our goals. A definite major purpose that is emotionalized will quickly manifest itself in our reality. The stronger we feel about something the sooner it will happen.

Hopefully, our life's goals will align with Dr. Hill's 12 Riches of Life. Here they are in the order he wrote them. You might notice that Financial Security is at the bottom of the list.

1. A Positive Mental Attitude
2. Sound Physical Health
3. Harmony in Human Relationships
4. Freedom from Fear
5. The Hope of Achievement
6. The Capacity for Faith
7. Willingness to Share One's Blessings
8. A Labor of Love
9. An Open Mind on All Subjects
10. Self-Discipline
11. The Capacity to Understand People
12. Financial Security

Although Dr. Hill didn't directly state this, you can probably determine your degree of satisfaction with your life by how your personal goals relate to Hill's 12 Riches of Life. Each is important. Not one is optional.

As an "experiment" of sorts, why not assign a percentage for each of the 12 Riches in your life now. Let the percentage represent how present each is today. Make sure they total 100% when you are finished. Now, sit back and reflect on which of the riches should be debited or credited to your "balance." Strive for a positive balance, and you will be a happier, more productive you who can not only swing on a star, but be far better off than you are right now.

REFLECTION
He who every morning plans the transactions of the day and follows out that plan carries a thread that will guide him through the labyrinth of the most busy day.
–VICTOR HUGO

$\mathcal{L}esson$ 25

*You must believe that what you want will
happen, and you must take the necessary
action to ensure it.*

—NAPOLEON HILL

In Chapter 8 of *Think and Grow Rich*, Napoleon Hill details
the legacy of freedom that the 56 signers of the Declaration of
Independence bequeathed to every American living today.
Our national July 4th Independence Day celebration is a time
to reflect on the characteristics of these fearless men who
persistently pursued their definite major purpose in the face of
strong adversities. However, each did so with unwavering
faith, strong personal initiative, and a corresponding positive
mental attitude. I ask myself, if we were among these men in
the meeting room, would we have signed the document? I
think not. Demanding immediacy with a "what's in it for me"
attitude would prevent any consensus being reached.

As we look back to look ahead, let's consider for a moment
what our lives would have been like if these men did not take
action. Ben Franklin's comment, "Either we hang together, or
hang separately" is a good statement to reflect on in today's
world. Ask yourself, what program do you want to follow?: 1)
the good for all program, or 2) the what's in it for me program.
Your answer will alert you as to whether or not your name
would have endorsed freedom for all.

Napoleon Hill states: "But, the greatest decision of all time, as
far as any American citizen is concerned, was reached in
Philadelphia, July 4, 1776, when fifty-six men signed their

names to a document, which they well knew would bring freedom to all Americans, or leave every one of the fifty-six hanging from a gallows!"

Let's remember our ancestors for the legacy of freedom that was their gift to us. In doing so may we become more generous with our time, talent, and treasure as we too strive to make this world a better place. We can begin right now by reciting Napoleon Hill's self-confidence formula that appears in Chapter 3 of *Think and Grow Rich*. Read daily, this formula strengthens our positive intentions to go out and be of service to those needing help.

REFLECTION
To improve the golden moment of opportunity and catch the good that is within our reach is the great art of life.

–WILLIAM JAMES

Lesson 26

Copy the following statement and put it where you'll see it the first thing in the morning and the last thing at night: I have a definite major purpose, and it is my duty to transform this purpose into reality. Therefore, I will develop the daily habit of taking action that will bring me closer to its attainment.

—NAPOLEON HILL

We've all heard the saying "it's music to my ears!" The meaning behind this statement is that we are happy about the message that has been received. Napoleon Hill understood the significance of music and the effect that it can have on people. In an early essay, he details the positive results that can be received just by listening to music that is harmonious. As Hill documents the potential benefits of music we can consider how music has enhanced our own lives. Musical selections have the capability of raising our emotions and our spirits. They can also calm our nerves, reduce stress, and create a certain ambiance for a special dinner or event.

In relationship to maintaining a positive mental attitude, music has great importance. While studying the 17 success principles that Dr. Hill outlines in his **PMA Science of Success Course,** I encourage students to match a song that "speaks" to them for each principle. Next, I suggest that they also select a song for an overture and one for a finale. When finished, they then can compile a CD for their personal listening pleasure of all 19 selections and listen to it daily to awaken their Positive Mental Attitude. In doing this exercise, students report that: 1) they have studied the 17 principles more in depth in order to choose the best song to correspond with the principle under study, and 2) that when they listen to the cd the lesson is repeated over again. According to W. Clement Stone, repetition is the key to thoroughly learning these principles. And, by taking the corresponding action in the creation of your "personalized" cd you are telling your subconscious mind that you mean business in regard to the integration of this success philosophy into your daily life. Try it, and see if it makes a difference for you too. Not only is it fun to do, but challenging as well.

REFLECTION
We cannot change the nature of a thought or of a truth, but, we can, as it were, guide the ship by moving the helm.
–PROFESSOR ELMER GATES

Lesson 27

When a group of individual minds are coordinated and function in harmony, the increased energy created through that alliance becomes available to every individual in the group.

—NAPOLEON HILL

When Dr. Hill put his imagination to work after a lecture he gave where only 13 people showed up in Canton, Ohio, he focused on turning an adversity into a benefit. Envisioning the number 13 in his mind, he asked himself what was significant about the number and how it could be interpreted as a good sign instead of a bad omen. Well, you can read below what he came up with, and it is a very positive outcome.

Today we have our Mastermind Online Club that is maintained through our website at www.naphill.org. I see this as a logical progression of the Thirteen Club. Our online club has been in existence since the year 2000, and the membership continues to grow. I am always amazed at the strong input and advice some of the long term members and charter members continue to give free of charge through their posts, as well as how little new members take advantage of the wisdom of the group. Many members just read what is posted, but that is insufficient. In order to create a dialog, a member must post questions and read responses. In this manner, a forum is created that allows for the give and take of a discussion group.

If you haven't joined already, why not join? Past postings are still available for your reading pleasure as well as the recordings of conference calls and our Vintage newsletters.

Even with these "perks" the ultimate benefit is in the discussion board wherein you can ask questions and receive responses from around the world. I believe that with a little modification, we can "adjust" Dr. Hill's Rules for the Thirteen Club, and also make them applicable to our Mastermind Online. Below are the proposed rules of membership. I am sure that if you follow them, you will be the better for it in every way.

Each member of the Mastermind Online Club must comply with the following program that Napoleon Hill authored himself after the initial ill-fated meeting that only 13 people attended:

1. Take and faithfully observe a pledge to form the habit of always rendering more service and better service than that for which he or she is paid.
2. Master and apply in his or her daily work, the 17 principles of success.
3. Cooperate with the other members of the club in assisting them in the application of the 17 principles of success in their daily work.
4. Start a savings account and add to it a certain definite pro rata of all earnings each week, this account not to be withdrawn for a period of five years.
5. Adopt and follow a personal budget system of control over expenditures.
6. Submit to a personal analysis every six months for the purpose of determining whether the member is advancing, standing still or going backward. Only those who show continuous growth, through assimilation of the club's educational program, may remain in the club.
7. Carry life insurance, in some approved company, in proportion to earning capacity.
8. Form a habit of prayer, and resort to that habit in whatever manner and at such times as the member may prefer.

9. Choose a definite purpose as a life work and create a definite plan for the achievement of that purpose.
10. Follow a program of collateral reading of books on subjects connected with the member's definite purpose in life, thereby taking advantage of that which others have discovered relating to that purpose.
11. Introduce at least one other person for membership in the Thirteen Club movement, thereby rendering to another the privilege of the benefits to be derived from the club.
12. Read Emerson's essay on the law of compensation once every six months.
13. Adopt the golden rule philosophy as the basis of all business and professional transactions.

REFLECTION

The meeting of two personalities is like the contact of two chemical substances: if there is a reaction, both are transformed.

–CARL JUNG

SHORT LESSONS ON LIFE
by Napoleon Hill

The sub-conscious mind will not be influenced by any suggestions made to it except those which are mixed with feeling or emotion.

Knowledge is of no value unless and until it is expressed in some form of useful service.

Lesson 28

*Positive and negative emotions cannot occupy the
mind at the same time.*

—NAPOLEON HILL

W. Clement Stone was a master motivator. Like Charles
Schwab, Stone was able to spread contagious enthusiasm
throughout his workforce and personal contacts. People
believed him because he took action and did what he
challenged others to do himself. Stone was Hill's best model
student and lived up to every expectation that Dr. Hill had of
an individual who internalized his philosophy of success for
his benefit as well as for the benefit of others.

How did Stone accomplish all he did? He himself gives us the
formula. He states that one should memorize, understand, and
repeat frequently: "What the mind can conceive and believe,
the mind can achieve." He clarifies that it's a form of self-
suggestion, a self-motivator to success. By programming your
mental attitude for success through autosuggestion, what you
condition yourself for soon becomes a part of you.
Consequently, you dare to aim higher.

I like to think of this as imprinting rather than self-suggestion.
In nature, we see animals following this practice. If it works in
the animal kingdom, of which we are part, it should work for
us—but even better because we can do it consciously whereas
the lower animals cannot. Think about it! What you think
about you become! When you think about success rather than
failure, when you think about happiness rather than sorrow,

when you think about faith rather than fear, you are imprinting expectations in your subconscious mind that your conscious mind sets out to find in your every day sensory world. How awesome is that? It's our personal buried treasure map! The fact that we can condition ourselves for success is, in itself, a miracle of mental awareness.

Now that we have the operating instructions that are the key to our success, we can truly become what we think about—so think good, lofty thoughts!

<u>REFLECTION</u>
We are shaped and fashioned by what we love.
—GOETHE

Lesson 29

> *Your imagination will become weak through inaction. It can be revived and made alert through use.*
>
> —NAPOLEON HILL

August usually is a hot month in the Midwest. During times like these our incentive to work dwindles and our productivity declines. Many people blame the heat, the absence of co-workers who are vacationing, and the high prices for everything and anything that goes wrong under the sun. Truthfully, if you look for a reason something can't be done you are bound to find five to ten good ones. Reasons like:

We never did this in the past.
People would complain.
It costs too much.
We can't be sure of its marketability.
We are too shorthanded to complete the task.
It's not what we as a company are about.
Where will we get the money to fund it?
What if it doesn't take off?
Run it by James, but I'm sure he won't like it.
How can you possibly fit this in, when you are still behind?

You get the picture. Creativity and imagination nipped in the bud. Perhaps in August, when the heat is at its hottest everyone longs to do something different—if just for awhile. Wouldn't it be neat if the month of August were named Creativity Month, and employees could spark their interest by taking part in a project of their choice that is imaginative and unusual. This would leave the other 11 months open for more mundane things, but always August would be for the budding entrepreneur who thinks that with a little ingenuity the company could be improved. To appease the higher ups, September could be designated Performance Month.

Creativity and imagination might be looked at like the juice of the soul. A writer, Julia Cameron, discusses the significance of taking time for yourself to refuel your inner artist—she calls these weekly dates with yourself doing something you love Artist's Dates. It would be wise for management everywhere to do likewise. Time for brainstorming and daydreaming fuels the productivity of the future. Ask yourself how kitty litter, Eskimo pies, Whoppers, and e-books came to be if not through conscious day-dreaming. Day-dreaming might be defined as time wasted or it might also be defined as truth in advance. Take your pick. Motivate yourself first so that you can motivate others. Consider if you need to break away from the traditional in order to refuel so that you can then go full speed ahead. Remember, when you get the man right, your world will be right!

REFLECTION
The imagination should be allowed a certain amount of time to browse around.
–THOMAS MERTON

Lesson 30

*Fear is the most costly of all the human emotions,
even though most fears have no foundation in fact.*
—NAPOLEON HILL

Dr. Napoleon Hill lists the seven basic fears. They are: fear of poverty, fear of ill health, fear of criticism, fear of the loss of love, fear of old age, fear of the loss of liberty, and fear of death. When discussing these fears, he cautions us to remember that fears are nothing more than states of mind that are always subject to our control and direction. As we work toward taking possession of our own mind, we learn the significance of keeping a positive mental attitude and also focusing on our definite major purpose. The more we attain control of our mind, the more we can overcome our fears. When we are positive and focused, our fears recede.

W. Clement Stone knew full well that fears are mainly emotional and not rational. In order to overcome the fear involved in selling, Stone discovered that taking action can put fear on the back burner. When we are fearful, we are not faithful. Fear is the opposite of faith, and faith without works is dead. In order to bring faith to the forefront we must be action oriented, and by taking action we reduce our fears in size one by one.

W. Clement Stone created the mantra "Do it now!" as a self-starter. He states that he did this because he found that action would dispel fear. He adds that emotions are not subject to reason, but they're always subject to action. So, by repeating

"Do it now!" to yourself over and over, you are commanding yourself to action. This autosuggestion works well when we are stopped in our tracks due to something that causes us to be fearful. By doing it now, we develop the persistence we need to keep going when we would rather quit. Oddly enough, it is not the smartest person who often reaches the goal, but the most persistent one. Just by doing it now, you can add a little more mileage to your journey toward your goal, and persistence will become something that will enable you to complete the journey. Remember, "Do it now!" today and every day. When you do it now, you won't wonder what might have been. Persistence together with action will give you the extra momentum to succeed.

<u>REFLECTION</u>
I steer my bark with Hope ahead and Fear astern.
–THOMAS JEFFERSON

Lesson 31

In every soul there has been deposited the seed of a great future, but that seed will never germinate—much less grow to maturity—except through the rendering of useful service.

—NAPOLEON HILL

We do not have to have everything in place in order to succeed, just the determination, willingness, and persistence to make it happen—and some Divine help never hurts too.

As President of the Chicago Boys Club, Stone took it upon himself to make a difference in the lives of boys with limited opportunities because he knew this was where he **could** make a difference. Raised in a single parent household, Stone knew firsthand what kids could be up against. He decided to engage these club members actively and asked what it was they wanted to do. By doing this, Stone managed to cultivate their interest and next supply them with the motivation and the means to develop themselves further in school and in work. The plan worked and Stone was eager to report that through effort, the boys were able to catch up with their more advanced and advantaged peers in no time.

Together with Napoleon Hill, Stone undertook a prison rehabilitation program called *PMA Science of Success.* This program led prisoners through the Positive Mental Attitude Course that was created by Hill and Stone when the two were in partnership. This course is still being taught today nationwide. The type of generosity displayed by Mr. Stone, and the carryover it has yet today in prison programs makes one applaud the magnitude of his dreams. Without him taking the personal initiative to institute these programs in his lifetime, people living today would have remained untouched. The beauty of a dream is not that it only serves the individual who realizes it, but that it takes on a life of its own and extends the life of the dreamer. We remember Mr. Stone today not for his wealth, but for the magnitude of his generosity that lives yet today in the reform programs he began decades ago.

REFLECTION
If your actions inspire others to dream more, learn more, do more and become more, you are a leader.
–JOHN QUINCY ADAMS

Lesson 32

The secret of getting things done is to act. The way to success is organized thinking followed by action! action! action!

—NAPOLEON HILL

Every fall, our thoughts turn toward education as schools reopen after summer vacation. Learning does not stop at the schoolhouse door or at graduation. Lifelong learning is the only vehicle to positive growth and change that is available to all. As lifelong learners, our thoughts too should turn toward reinvigorating our minds and hearts with the timeless philosophy of Napoleon Hill. Each day is a new beginning and a new opportunity to create the person we desire to become. Remember, life isn't finished with us until we are finished with life.

Everyone begins at the beginning. Dr. Hill was no exception. He positioned himself for future success by conditioning his mind with positive attitudes toward success. Laying the foundation is important. Have an idea, create a plan for its achievement, and work the plan. Thoughts + Action = SUCCESS.

Do you have a plan? Have you written it down? Do you read it several times daily? Are you conditioning your subconscious mind to open the door when opportunity knocks? Be continually aware that what we think about we become. Think about success. Think about opportunities. Think about positive responses to negative world conditions. Position yourself for greatness and then make it so! We truly are the creators of our future. Why not create a positive one?

As all students know, after the lesson comes the assignment. Your assignment is to write down your plan, read it daily until it crystallizes in your subconscious mind, and simultaneously act on the plan however you are able. Dig into your plan deeper and deeper and before you know it you will be living the life you like.

<u>REFLECTION</u>
The highest reward for man's toil is not what he gets for it, but what he becomes by it.

–JOHN RUSKIN

Lesson 33

All your successes and failures are the result of habits you have formed.

—NAPOLEON HILL

Procrastination is a subversive thief that slowly steals your dreams of success. Little by little this cunning foe robs you of your potential to reach higher and higher dreams. When we allow our life to be whittled down to nothingness because of our willingness to put off until tomorrow what we can do today, we trade our destiny for sloth.

Looking at procrastination from the perspective of missed opportunities of our own creation gives us a different vantage point from which to view life's failures. We create our destiny one day at a time by the thoughts that we think and the choices that we make. If we delay our choices, we will never reach our optimum goal. Choice making followed by positive action is the substance of dreams come true. Determining what and when we want to do something in advance hedges our chances for success. Waiting until the muse strikes us or waiting for the perfect time and place are sure recipes for failure. Accepting the fact that nothing is perfect destroys the belief that our best opportunity must align with the stars. The best time is now, the best day is today, and the best tools are what we have at our disposal this very minute. Knowing this, we can show procrastination the door. Emerson reminds us to do the thing and we shall have the power. This affirmation should be recited daily in order to condition our mind for success.

In the book *Poems that Inspire You to Think and Grow Rich* there is a quotation from William Shakespeare that merits repeating:

> There is a tide in the affairs of men,
> Which, taken at the flood, leads on to fortune;
> Omitted, all the voyage of their life
> Is bound in shallows and in miseries.
> On such a full sea are we now afloat;
> And we must take the current when it serves,
> Or lose our ventures.
>
> —WILLIAM SHAKESPEARE

Do you want to be captain at the helm of your life, or do you want to be shipwrecked on life's shoals? Procrastinators miss the boat every time. Only those who do it now will arrive at their dreams on schedule. Take the current and move forward full speed ahead!

REFLECTION
He who has begun, has the work half done.

—HORACE

Lesson 34

*That which you think today becomes that which
you are tomorrow.*

—NAPOLEON HILL

PMA SHAPE-UP PLAN
*17 simple action steps to get you in a
positive frame of mind in no time!*

The Plan: Staying positive requires regular use of your mental muscles. If you want to get in perfect PMA conditioning, you need to focus on one or more of the 17 Principles daily. By spending just 15 to 30 minutes per day on these PMA exercises, you will prove to yourself that being positive does make a difference in your lifestyle in just a matter of days—17 days to be exact. Through this mental strengthening routine you will acquire more positive characteristics than you ever thought possible.

The Payoff: If you do these 17 simple exercises, one per day, I promise you a Positive Mental Attitude that will deliver results immediately. Start now and create a more positive you in just 17 steps.

Day 1: Develop a Definite Purpose.
Start now. Select something that you want to accomplish within these next 17 days. Write down this goal in your own handwriting on a 4 x 6 inch note card. State your goal as if you have already accomplished it. For example, "I dress for success." "I have $500 of savings in my bank account." "I eat

and drink only those things that promote my best health." "I am doing work that reflects my right livelihood." "I walk three miles daily." You get the idea. Write down your definite purpose now. Next, on this same card, document daily the action that you have taken toward this goal. For example, each day after you walk three miles, login your entry on the card by writing the date and the miles walked. Track your success.

Day 2: Establish a Master Mind Alliance.
Select a friend, co-worker, email partner, family member, or an "invisible" guide, who you share your progress with regarding the goal you have established. Make it a formal daily contact at an established time for the next two weeks. It need not be a long meeting. Just "meet" for a few minutes daily to make certain that you remain on track. This person will become your personal coach, your promoter, your pacesetter in keeping you on the straight and narrow track toward your goal. On the second note card, write down the name of the person you selected to be in your Master Mind Alliance. Below the name, track your daily progress by recording the dates and times that you maintained contact with your personal success coach.

Day 3: Applied Faith.
Create 10 personal affirmations around your definite major purpose and write these affirmations on the third note card. Repeat several times daily by reading your affirmations out loud and internalizing the message. For example, using the goal of "I walk three miles daily," possible personal affirmations are:

> I walk three miles daily without exception.
> I feel healthy, happy, and terrific after my daily three mile walk.
> I enjoy being outside in the fresh air during my daily three mile walk.
> I benefit physically by my daily three mile walk by burning calories.

I benefit socially during my daily three mile walk by talking to fellow trekkers.

I benefit spiritually during my daily three mile walk by communing with nature.

I benefit mentally during my daily three mile walk by clearing my mind of troublesome worries.

I benefit emotionally during my daily three mile walk by reducing built up stress through regular exercise.

I benefit myself by toning my muscles during my daily three mile walk.

I benefit my neighbor during my daily three mile walk by supporting his/her efforts as well.

Remember to record your progress.

Day 4: Going the Extra Mile.

Perform a random act of kindness on the way to or from work. Do something that you do for no return on your investment. Do good because you choose to do good. Pay someone's toll behind you, speak positively about a person whom you dislike, pack a lunch for a family member who is short on time, run an errand or two for an individual with too many duties, or volunteer to help a cause in your community. Expect no return on your services. Just put the good that you do out to the Universe, and notice how the Universe repays you many times over. Record your good deed on your fourth note card. You may add additional good deeds as you complete them.

Day 5: Pleasing Personality.

Today is your day! Decide to do something luxurious for yourself. Spend time pampering the person you know best— YOU! Invest in you, and the investment will pay off. Create a time and space that accommodate you and then treat yourself to a time spent on your interests. Read a favorite book, take a hot bath, swing in a hammock for an hour, brew refreshing ice tea, or just kick back and watch a favorite old movie. But, do it because you want to, not because it is on your to-do list. Record your activity on the fifth note card and note your reaction as well. Repeat as needed.

Day 6: Personal Initiative.
Remember all those "I'll do it when I get around to it" promises that you made to yourself? Well, today you will get around to doing one of those things on the long to-do list. Jump in and clean a closet, file those papers, polish the silver, wax the floor, or anything else that is pestering you to complete. Set a timer for 1 hour and begin the project. Don't think about it, don't plan it, don't postpone it, just accomplish it. Now, on note card 6 list the project you just completed and cross it off the list. Underneath the newly finished project, add the next one to be done when you have a spare hour or two. There is great satisfaction in transferring your thoughts into action that is energized. We hold the power to transform our intentions into reality. **Do It NOW!**

REFLECTION

Nor I—nor anyone else, can travel that road for you. You must travel it yourself.

–WALT WHITMAN

Lesson 35

No one who is unwilling to make personal sacrifices achieves great success. All positive habits are the product of willpower directed toward the attainment of definite goals.

—NAPOLEON HILL

PART 2 OF PMA SHAPE-UP PLAN

17 simple action steps to get you in a positive frame of mind in no time!

Day 7: Positive Mental Attitude.

Decide to be positive in everything you do today. Don't overwhelm yourself, however, just be positive second by second, minute by minute, and the hours and the day will take care of themselves. Just make a conscious effort to use positive thoughts, words, and actions as you progress through the day. Think before you speak and act in order to remind yourself that today is going to be a Positive Mental Attitude Day. Let nothing or no one divert you from your purpose. On note card number 7, record a statement about how maintaining a positive mental attitude colored your outlook on the day. We get what we expect to get. Expect the best.

Day 8: Enthusiasm.

Become childlike. Recall something that you enjoyed doing or experiencing as a child. It could be bike riding or eating a favorite ice cream cone. Relive that experience and feel the enthusiasm grow again inside of you. Anticipate what it is that you are about to experience, and tell yourself that you will have a truly joyful memory or episode. Decide to be enthusiastic and you will be enthusiastic. We can control our emotions, and enthusiasm allows us to program ourselves for a successful experience. Enthusiasm kindles the fire that fuels our definite major purpose. Get yourself a burning desire and keep it burning with enthusiasm. On note card number 8, list several things that you have been enthusiastic about during your life. Relive these memories and enjoy the feelings of pleasure accompanied with them. Now, transfer this enthusiasm to your new goal and anticipate the same results. Record your findings.

Day 9: Self-Discipline.
You have heard about diets and fasting. About focusing on something until it is yours. About denying yourself small things until you can purchase the big item that you really want. Well, that is what self-discipline is all about. It is good to recognize that our mind plays tricks on us and attempts to divert us from achieving our goal when it looks too much like work. The principle of self-discipline teaches us how to nip this problem in the bud. Exhibit self-discipline in the area of your definite major purpose and sooner versus later you will have the outcome that you desire. Today, discipline yourself to work on your definite major purpose for an extended period of time. Say **no** to the "ego" when it says: "Let's do lunch," or "Let's take a nap." Instead, say that all these things are okay, but you won't do them now. Rather, you will use self-discipline to work on your goal first and foremost. On note card number 9, write down ten ways you attempt to distract yourself from your definite major purpose. Sometimes we stall our own best efforts by not practicing self-discipline. Don't let the lack of self-discipline have victory over you.

Day 10: Accurate Thinking.
We live in an elaborate world. Things are confusing. It is difficult to analyze everything prior to making decisions. However, just for today let's evaluate the benefit of doing something that we do daily. For example, maybe you leave for

work at a peak traffic time. Have you considered how much time you could save by leaving earlier or even later than usual? Consider the benefits of planning your day around the off-schedules of others. Does lunch have to be at noon, and quitting time at 5:00? On note card number 10, create the time schedule of your day as it currently exists. Now using accurate thinking, analyze your day hour by hour and see if you currently are using the most effective plan. Where can you make changes that will enhance the quality and quantity of time spent? Finally, create a new schedule for yourself showing how your new awareness has changed the manner in which you spend or allocate your time.

Day 11: Controlled Attention.
Thoughts are things. We bring into being that which we think about. We get what we focus on in life. By controlling our attention, we control our outcomes. An old saying goes, "When the student is ready, the teacher will come." By focusing our attention on what it is we want in life, we are keeping it off the things that we do not want. Use note card number 11 to designate an area in your life that you are going to focus on for the purpose of improving that area. It can be financial, spiritual, mental, physical, or emotional in nature. Select one and decide that you are going to pay close attention to that area today in order to understand how you are creating your reality in that one area. If it is financial, watch your spending for one day and record your transactions. If it is spiritual, note how you connect with Infinite Intelligence. If it is mental, ask yourself how you continually increase your storehouse of knowledge. If it is physical, note how you treat your physical body. Or, if it is emotional, determine whether you control or are controlled by your emotions. Raise your level of awareness about how you use Controlled Attention.

Day 12: Teamwork.
Organize a small activity for fun. Involve several people. They can be family, co-workers, friends, or members of a group. Get

together prior to the event to brainstorm (email, phone, in-person) the purpose of the activity and what needs to be done before the event can occur. For example, it might be a small family reunion. In order for the reunion to be a success, the work must be distributed. Have individuals sign-up for various tasks. Watch what teamwork can accomplish that you could not do as effectively alone. Now, on note card number 12, list ten ways you can benefit by using teamwork in your life. Every job can be divided into a series of tasks. Teams make the tasks easy to do, and no one feels overburdened. How can you share the load with someone else?

REFLECTION
God gives every bird its food, but He does not throw it into the nest.

–J. G. HOLLAND

Lesson 36

Who told you "It couldn't be done?" And, what
great achievement has he to his credit that
qualifies him to judge your ability?

—NAPOLEON HILL

PART 3 OF PMA SHAPE-UP PLAN
17 simple action steps to get you in a
positive frame of mind in no time!

Day 13: Learning from Adversity and Defeat.

Feeling overwhelmed? Are things not headed in the right direction? Do you feel as if you have failed at something that you attempted to do? Do you have a sense of inadequacy or a sense of loss? What can we learn from this? Spend a few moments recalling a failure that you experienced several years ago. Look at both side of the issue. Certainly, there were losses, but there were also gains. Now, focus on the benefits that came to you because of this failure. That's correct. The benefits are what you need to find buried in the defeat. If you look hard enough, and critically analyze the failure long enough, you will find the seed for an equal or equivalent benefit. Start looking. On note card number 13, recall a failure. List the adversities that occurred because of this failure, and next list the benefits. "Every adversity and defeat carries with it the seed of an equal or equivalent benefit." Find the rose among the thorns and you will be on the road to finding personal success.

Day 14: Creative Vision.

Have fun. Create something. Be artistic and let the child within you play freely. Do something that you enjoy doing for the sheer joy of doing it. Be self-actualizing. Draw, paint, sculpt, color, or just design something. After you complete your artistic creation, take a snapshot of it and attach it to note card number 14. Admire your creativity and handiwork.

Day 15: Maintenance of Sound Health.

You know the risks of not living a healthy lifestyle. What about the benefits? Do you drink eight glasses of water per day? Do you eat food that promotes your optimum health? Average 8 hours of sleep per night? Practice renewal time for your mind, body, and spirit? Why not? On note card number 15, select an area of focus that will improve your physical health. Decide on one area of improvement and stick to it for a minimum of 21 days. After the 21st day, your routine will become a habit. Document each day that you stayed with the program.

Day 16: Budgeting Time and Money.

Where you spend your time and your money is a strong indicator of where you will end up years from now. Know where you are overspending, where you should save, and how you can make improvements in both areas. On note card 16, examine how you spend your 8 hours of "free" time each day. Is it sleeping, watching T.V., socializing, or studying, reflecting, and doing things related to your definite major purpose? If too much time is spent on non-related things, you will not accomplish that which you have set out to accomplish in Day 1. Look back and then look ahead. You control your time. Time does not control you. Take possession of it.

Day 17: Cosmic Habitforce.

We are the sum and substance of the habits that we have forged for ourselves throughout life. Examine your habits. Which ones do you control and which ones control you? Habits are at first cobwebs and then cables. Know how to undo a bad habit and how to add a good habit. On note card 17, examine the daily habits that you perform. Do these habits serve you, or do they control you? Unlock the key to your true potential by forging new habits that serve you in your quest for success. On the front side of the note card, list your beneficial habits. On the backside of the note card, list your detrimental habits. Now begin to accentuate the positive and eliminate the negative. When you overcome a negative habit, cross it off the list permanently. When you accelerate a positive habit, give yourself a gold star. Soon the positive habits will be greater in number, and you will be the greater because you have strengthened your positive characteristics. A habit is learned and integrated into our daily system of doing things within 21 days. Dedicate 21 days to becoming an improved person, by adding just one positive habit. Think what you can do in a year!

Report Card:
There you have it! A daily schedule for success. **Success = Thoughts + Actions.** Without the "doing" there are no results. The best intention is not worth the least action. Put yourself on the success beam by doing success strengthening exercises! Your mental muscle power will accelerate your road to success. By shaping up, you will be making great strides on the road to success throughout the rest of the year.

<u>REFLECTION</u>
You cannot play symphonies until you
have first mastered the notes.

–DR. EDWARD L. KRAMER

SHORT LESSONS ON LIFE
by Napoleon Hill

School may enable a man to acquire much knowledge and assemble many useful facts, but schooling alone does not necessarily make a man educated. Education is self-acquired, and it comes through development and use of the mind, and in no other way.

Awaken the sleeping giant with you!

Lesson 37

*The master key to success lies in your capacity
to believe that you will succeed.*

—NAPOLEON HILL

Recently I had the opportunity to spend several hours with a person who indicates that Napoleon Hill's Philosophy is the ultimate factor in his life's success. Visiting his office filled with a lifetime of memorabilia, I couldn't help but notice that the walls were literally covered with images of this gentleman at various stages of his success. These images created a series of individual stills that became the storyboard of his life. As I looked at hundreds of photos, it gave me a rare opportunity to see a life develop due to the underlying influence of Napoleon Hill. By envisioning the POSITIVE SELF that Dr. Hill discusses, this man was able to set a higher standard above his existing reality. This "new reality" then became for him a point of destination in his not-too-distant future.

One of his success memories involves an organizational chart for the company that had just hired him. Once he was put on the payroll, the head of human resources took great pride in penciling him in at the very bottom of the chart and then handing it to him. Instead of crumbling it up and throwing it in the trash, this man took the chart to his garage "apartment" and placed it at the foot of his bed. Nightly, he studied it while engaging his creative imagination. At every opportunity he mentally envisioned himself climbing the organizational ladder at which he was labeled the bottom rung. Rather than being a deterrent to his advancement, this organizational chart became a visual image of inspiration for him that culminated in his ultimate success within that very company. Due in part to this visualization practice, within less than five years he went from hotel clerk to the general manager. Can't you just imagine the head of human resources wondering under his breath how this happened at all—and so quickly?

Well, if you're wondering too, you can just ask Jim Connelly and he will tell you straight up that there was no real magic to it! He followed the formula Dr. Hill created in *Think and Grow Rich* and used it to his advantage. He tells me that nothing less than success was always the result. This "magic" formula still exists today, and you too can find it in *Think and Grow Rich*. Just ask Jim if he believes it can still work. He will refer you to the "Six Ways to Turn Desires into Gold" located in Chapter Two of *Think and Grow Rich*, and let you be the judge.

REFLECTION
Live a great life where you are, and in the daily work you have to do, and greater works will surely find you out. Big things will come to you, asking to be done.

–WALLACE D. WATTLES

Lesson 38

Any dominating idea, plan or purpose held in the conscious mind through repetition of thought and emotionalized by a burning desire for its realization is taken over by the subconscious and acted upon through whatever natural and logical means may be available.

—NAPOLEON HILL

Your subconscious mind is a powerful mental magnet. Napoleon Hill's Philosophy of Success works more efficiently when you engage your subconscious mind in the learning process. Always advanced for his time, Dr. Hill recognized that the conscious mind was merely the tip of the iceberg. More advanced and more directly useful to students of success is the subconscious mind. This greater mind can be accessed through positive affirmations, meditation, repetition, and visualization. Visual images can accelerate the manifestation of personalized goals and objectives. Dr. Hill's famous epigram: "Whatever the mind can conceive and believe, the mind can achieve" works in conjunction with the subconscious mind. By repeating this famous saying, one becomes convinced that individuals can dream, affirm, and manifest personalized goals.

Dr. Hill states that: "You may voluntarily plant in your subconscious mind any plan, thought, or purpose which you desire to translate into its physical or monetary equivalent. The subconscious acts first on the dominating desires which have been mixed with emotional feeling, such as faith." The subconscious mind is the seat of the emotions and responds to either positively or negatively charged emotionalized ideas. The thinker controls the thoughts—good or bad; however, the subconscious mind programs the outcome. How does this work? Simply put, the subconscious mind is like a fertile garden. Seeds of greatness or seeds of despair can be sown. Sowing seeds of greatness will yield a garden full of beautiful outcomes, while sowing seeds of despair will yield the opposite. As soon as a person understands that "thoughts are things," the process can begin. Good thoughts can be planted in the subconscious mind and positive results can be harvested, and likewise bad thoughts can be planted and a crop of negative results will grow. Utilizing this process, it becomes obvious that success is achieved through a combination of good thoughts combined with good actions. By controlling one's thoughts, a person can control his destiny. Dr. Hill states that: "Everything which man creates begins in the form of a thought impulse."

A thought aligned with strong emotion has a quicker gateway to the subconscious mind than simply a thought without the attachment of an emotionalized feeling. Comparing emotionalized thought to the yeast that causes bread dough to rise, Dr. Hill explains that emotion is the action element that transforms thought into action. The metaphor of yeast is a good one because it works slowly but uniformly; and before a person realizes it, the dough has multiplied many times over its original size.

As you hand over your desires to your subconscious mind, you are planting the seeds of your desire and allowing the subconscious to take inner control, and transmute your desires into reality. A negative thought and a positive thought cannot exist in the subconscious mind simultaneously. They cancel one another out. By focusing on the positive emotions of desire, faith, love, sex, enthusiasm, romance and hope, one can avoid allowing the negative emotions of fear, jealousy, hatred, revenge, greed, superstition, and anger to take root and destroy the positive outlook. By disciplining the mind to only allow positive emotions to prevail, an individual conditions the mind so that negative emotions are not permitted to enter it.

As the subconscious mind is given its marching orders, it also serves as an intermediary between the mind of man and Infinite Intelligence. When a proposition is installed by a positively emotionalized thought in the subconscious mind, it next presents the message to the supra-conscious mind or Infinite Intelligence, and brings back a plan of action that when acted upon brings about the desired goal.

REFLECTION
Faith consists in believing when it is beyond
the power of reason to believe.

—VOLTAIRE

SHORT LESSONS ON LIFE
by *Napoleon Hill*

*No person may be sure of success, no matter
what may be his calling, without applying
this principle of giving before trying to get!
Failure to apply this principle will render
practically useless every other principle for
the successful marketing of personal
services.*

*Hatred spreads like wild weeds in a garden,
without cultivation. Love must be nursed
and cultivated or it will perish of
starvation.*

Lesson 39

*Think about the fact that you have complete
control over but one thing—the power of your own
thoughts. You can clear the mental cobwebs of
negative passions, emotions, feelings, tendencies,
prejudices, beliefs and habits by consciously
developing their positive opposites.*
—NAPOLEON HILL

In writing on Applied Faith, Dr. Hill states: "We are what we are, and where we are, because of the dominating thoughts we have permitted to dwell in our own minds." As an individual works to clear the mind of negative thoughts, the mind is being prepared for an influx of Infinite Intelligence. This conditioning is essential before you can acquire an active faith that will aid in assisting you in accepting the guidance of Infinite Intelligence. The subconscious mind is the gateway to Infinite Intelligence, but it must be prepared as a garden is prepared before the seeds can be planted. In order to keep this gateway open, you must first mentally picture what you want. This mental imagery combined with applied faith will begin the germination of the seed of your desire.

Constantly remind the subconscious mind what it is you want, by repeating short, positive affirmations in the present tense. These affirmations should be stated as if the end result has already occurred. Next, continually hold positive thoughts regarding your goal and put into action steps that will carry you in the direction or realization of this goal. Finally, offer prayers of gratitude to Infinite Intelligence for the attainment of this goal as if it has already been accomplished. Some individuals like to call this "truth in advance." It works because your subconscious mind operates best in the present tense. If you pray for something in the future, your subconscious mind will register the thought that this result does not need to happen now, but in some future time. Offer expressions of gratitude and thanksgiving for what you have already received whether these things have manifested or not in your current, present reality. Infinite Intelligence will offer up a plan to you for the manifestation of your desire provided that your desire does not violate the rights of others. Follow this plan and it will lead you to your definite major purpose. Once received, give back for what you have been given. The Universe expects a return on its investment just as you do.

Gardeners understand this Law of Abundance when they reap the crop that they have sown. Single seeds that were sown now become multiplied many times over. A tomato does not produce one seed, but hundreds of seeds for the profitable gardener. Nature practices the Law of Abundance. You reap what you plant in your subconscious mind—good or bad—because this fertile ground does not distinguish. Rather, it only follows your emotionalized marching orders. In conclusion, your mind works like a magnet and draws like things to you. Send out positive thoughts and your subconscious mind will draw rather than repel likeminded thoughts to you—riches, prosperity, health, and all the good things in life. Conversely, negative thoughts feed and multiply upon themselves too. Condition your magnet for positive attraction, and feel the goodness flow into your life. Do not accept failure, poverty, ill-health, superstition, and all the ills of the world. These ills do not have to be part of your life program. Rather, tune your subconscious mind like a highly receptive radio that hones in on the exact station you want to receive. Program your subconscious mind for success and you will have it. Accept nothing less.

In the Midwestern United States, October is a prime month to begin your homework on the subconscious mind. Nature shows us her abundance via the colorful leaves, bountiful harvest, and Indian Summer days. Nurture your subconscious mind now to deliver your most deserved gifts right on schedule. Begin by utilizing some of the creative suggestions contained in this book. Create your bountiful harvest now and recognize the magnificent power within you!

Conceive It–Believe It–Achieve It.

<u>REFLECTION</u>

To will is to select a goal, determine a course
of action that will bring one to that goal, and
then hold to that action till the goal is reached.
The key is action.

–MICHAEL HANSON

SHORT LESSONS ON LIFE
by Napoleon Hill

*Defeat should be looked upon in precisely
the same manner that one accepts the
unpleasant experience of physical pain, for
it is obvious that physical pain is nature's
way of informing one that something needs
attention and correction. Pain, therefore,
may be a blessing and not a curse!*

*The most beneficial of all prayers are those
we offer as an expression of gratitude for
the blessings we already have.*

Lesson 40

Today is the first day of the rest of your life. Are you satisfied with where you are and the direction you are going? If not, take control of your life and change whatever needs to be changed. You and only you have the power to do this. You can change your world!

—NAPOLEON HILL

Consider for a moment how beneficial it is to have an entire season set aside to give thanks for the bounty that we have received throughout the year. Reflecting on the things and people we are grateful for can renew our spirits, heighten our awareness, and motivate us to continue to do good things for ourselves and others. Also, this season can provide us with an opportunity to undo any wrongs that we may have committed intentionally or unintentionally. Forgiveness allows us the opportunity to unburden ourselves of baggage that we no longer need to carry on our life's journey. Most importantly too, gratitude can only be appreciated when we consider what ingratitude looks like.

When examined closely, this gratitude coin has two sides. The "tails" side can be called self-pity and it can pull us down into the proverbial dumps just as much as the gratitude side of the coin can raise our spirits. Why do we allow ourselves to dwell on the darker moments of life as often as or even more often than we do on the lighter side? Could it be so that we can have a comparative yardstick with which to measure the good that has been bestowed upon us? Could it be to feel the full range of our emotions? Or perhaps it's to acknowledge that we are blessed with the right to choose our own thoughts? Regardless of the reasons, our thoughts—good or bad—color our lives and determine our outcomes. This is the important fact to remember.

Napoleon Hill oftentimes looks on the dark side of life to see the light. In his writings he details why the act of forgiving is more beneficial to the person doing the forgiving than to the person who is the beneficiary. The often overlooked benefit of forgiveness can cause us to reap additional rewards just by practicing the Golden Rule. Surely, the world is in need of this concept now more than ever before.

Why not decide right here, right now to forgive someone who is in need of forgiveness from you? Make your mind up to forgive them and to be done with it. Don't carry the burden any longer. Call the person, write a note, or pay them a short visit for the purpose of setting the issue right between you. And then just do it.

Don't you feel a lightness of being after you have finished? Well, that's just the loss of the additional weight that you have been carrying around with you unnecessarily until you decided to forgive. It's a nice feeling to lose all those psychic pounds of stored resentment, right? And, you didn't even have to change your eating habits! Forgive and forget to raise your spirits!

REFLECTION
When an archer misses the mark, he turns and looks for the fault within himself. Failure to hit the bull's-eye is never the fault of the target. To improve your aim—improve yourself.
–GILBERT ARLAND

Lesson 41

Successful people know precisely what they want, have a plan for getting it, believe in their ability to get it, and devote a major portion of their time to acquiring it.

—NAPOLEON HILL

Time is our most valuable commodity. It is imperative that we use it wisely. Each of us has eight hours for sleep, eight hours for earning a living, and eight remaining hours for recreation or some other form of dedication to our definite major purpose. Napoleon Hill tells us that the eight "personal" hours are the most significant ones because these will either make or break us as we strive toward our life's goal. This is not to say that we need to continue to feverishly work another job or take home our current job to achieve the elusive success that we have set as our personal bull's-eye. Rather, we need to work smarter not longer. We need to step out so that we can show up for our daily duties. We need, in simple terminology, to recharge our batteries before we burn out.

During the working day, our resources are depleted and we need to replenish what we have drained from ourselves. Doing more of the same does not enhance our personal resources, but rather diminishes them further. What is needed is a change of pace, something new, intriguing and different that will captivate our imagination and restore our equilibrium. For each of us this "something" is different, but we know internally what renews our spirit and gives us strength for the future. It may be a simple walk, a leisurely dinner, an hour with a book, a session with our pets, or just taking in a movie. This time spent in diversion enables us to relax and renew ourselves so that we do not experience the let-down of burn out.

Neglecting this aspect of ourselves can bring about disastrous results. We begin to shut down our imagination, creativity, and intuition because we are blocking those aspects of ourselves with a distorted work ethic. Closing off portions of our identity creates lack rather than abundance. Therefore, we must be mindful that we listen to our needs and react to them in a timely fashion. When our body cries out for recreation, downtime, and personal renewal it is not a good idea to postpone the need. Like sleep, food, and water, time for renewal is a very present need that does not deter us from our goals, but rather adds fuel for the journey.

What are you turning a deaf ear toward in your life right now? Consider listening for a change, and give yourself the opportunity to enjoy the time that you so richly deserve and like magic the riches will come back to you full circle. Time spent on you is not wasted. Time spent on yourself is the best investment in your future. Make sure you keep the date!

REFLECTION
When the well is dry, we know the
worth of water.
–BENJAMIN FRANKLIN

Lesson 42

*All things are possible to the person who
believes they are possible.*

—NAPOLEON HILL

November is the season of gratitude, of gift giving and extending kindnesses. Small, heartfelt tokens of affection are shared among family members and friends, business associates and employers, youngsters and adults. But, you may ask, what good does all this goodwill do for the giver? Why is it better to give than to receive? Napoleon Hill knew the answer to this seasonal question years ago. If here today, he would tell you that the aroma of the flowers stays on the hands of the giver. Simply put, this means that the gift and the giver are never truly separated. That is why Dr. Hill feels it is so important to express prayers of gratitude to Infinite Intelligence. In giving we also receive. The gift always comes full circle.

Dr. Hill suggested a prayer or creed to be recited daily to attract our definite major purpose into our lives. Below is the prayer as Dr. Hill wrote it. Why not recite this prayer at this year's Thanksgiving Dinner? Afterward, allow each of your guests to recall what they are grateful for, and then remind everyone that everything we have in this life is a gift from our Divine Creator. May we always honor the Giver and possess the wisdom to appreciate the wonderful gifts bestowed upon us in our lifetimes.

Life is our greatest gift and well worth remembering as we gather together to give thanks. Peace and Prosperity to you and yours this month of thanksgiving.

THE GRATITUDE PRAYER
by Napoleon Hill

I give thanks daily, not for mere riches, but for wisdom with which to recognize, embrace, and properly use the great abundance of riches I now have at my command. I have no enemies because I injure no man for any cause, but I try to benefit all with whom I come in contact by teaching them the way to enduring riches. I have more material wealth than I need because I am free from greed and covet only the material things I can use while I live.

<u>REFLECTION</u>
All the beautiful sentiments in the world weigh less than a simple lovely action.
–JAMES RUSSELL LOWELL

Lesson 43

Render more and better service than that for which you are paid and sooner or later you'll receive compound interest on compound interest from your investment. It is inevitable that every seed of service you sow will multiply and come back to you in overwhelming abundance.

—NAPOLEON HILL

Napoleon Hill's Gratitude Prayer is a testimonial to his strong belief in Applied Faith. He reassures students of his philosophy that if you repeat this prayer daily in alignment with your definite major purpose, marvelous things will begin to occur in your life. Why is this so? Let's see if we can begin to analyze the reasons this gratitude prayer can work so miraculously in our everyday lives.

First, this prayer is a prayer of thankfulness, not of petition. When praying this prayer, the individual is not requesting anything, but more importantly honoring and giving thanks for that which has already been received. This works to focus the person on the abundance that already exists and also to express to Infinite Intelligence thoughts of gratefulness for having been given so much so freely. When we look to the good in our lives, it is difficult to focus on the bad. In being grateful, you cannot also simultaneously bemoan a lack. Gratitude shines the spotlight on the good, while diminishing the bad. The age-old adage, "You get what you focus on," seems to be applicable here.

Second, this prayer emphasizes the importance of going the extra mile by stating a desire to share the way to enduring riches with all whom the person comes into contact. This sharing is freely done, because the person doing the praying knows that the Universe strongly supports the Law of Compensation. "What goes around comes around" is often an expression used to indicate that what you put out you, in turn, receive. Putting out good thoughts via prayers of gratitude causes good thoughts to return to you in kind.

Third, by focusing on goodness the person creates a positive environment for the mind. Good outcomes are preceded by positive thoughts. Since thoughts are things, thinking good thoughts helps to create a positive cycle of thoughts and outcomes. Think good things and experience good outcomes. Remember, you reap what you sow.

Fourth, by acknowledging that everything that is needed is already possessed, the person again is casting bread upon the waters knowing that it will be multiplied when returned. Nothing diminishes a person like worry. By refusing to worry, a person is able to control the mental state he decides to be in. When you control your state of mind, you can control your future. All this is accomplished by knowing that you already possess the "whatever" it is that you need. There is no lack. All good things come to those who expect them!

Fifth, repeating this prayer daily with enthusiasm allows the message to enter into your subconscious mind. The subconscious mind knows no right from wrong, but it does understand an emotionalized command when it is given one. Through repetition, the prayer conditions the mind for focusing on positive outcomes.

Sixth, Infinite Intelligence is grateful when a "Thank You" is expressed. For example, when someone thanks you for a favor or for some assistance, this considerate act naturally makes you want to do even more for that person. The "Thank You" sets up a positive regard for that person and causes the listener to want to continue to give. It works the same way with Infinite Intelligence.

Seventh, being thankful is courteous and contagious. Instead of complaining, find something to be thankful about and notice the difference in your outlook. Roses bloom where weeds once grew.

Eighth, as you condition your mind to being thankful, it will attract more goodness to you. Like attracts like. Ever notice a new car on the road, and then buy one? Immediately, you begin to see this car everywhere. That's how focus works. You find what you look for. Look for and acknowledge the good.

Ninth, as you take the best you can leave the rest. Focusing on the good reinforces the good. The bad departs due to lack of attention. You decide what you want to have in your life.

Tenth, you should do good because doing good is the right thing to do. In giving thanks, we accentuate the positive, that is, we do good. Good promotes good and begins a cycle of a self-fulfilling prophesy. Do good. It IS the right thing to do. Let your little light shine and soon it will eliminate the darkness.

Here are the basic steps to abundance through Dr. Hill's Gratitude Prayer:
1. Read the prayer daily.
2. Relate the prayer to your daily existence.
3. Assimilate the message into your own life. That is, incorporate the positive outlook into your own frame of mind.
4. Apply the technique of looking for many things to be grateful for in your daily life. A beautiful sunrise, a colorful autumn leaf, the cool crisp morning air, an exquisite rose, a helping hand, a sincere friend in time of need, an unexpected bonus at work, a devoted pet, and a favorite song are all reasons to be grateful.

5. Repeat the process daily beginning with step number one.
6. Notice the difference in your life. Make sure that you write down the highlights in your journal so that you can document the change!

<u>REFLECTION</u>
I would maintain that thanks are the highest form of thought, and that gratitude is happiness doubled by wonder.

–G. K. CHESTERTON

Lesson 44

Decide what kind of person you want to be, and develop positive traits by emulating others you admire. Replace bad habits with good ones and focus your mind on positive thoughts.

—NAPOLEON HILL

Dr. Hill discusses the significance of promoting yourself to a higher position. Every person needs to work on self-promotion through the enhancement of individual skills. Learning about the 17 success principles improves one's life in all the areas of personal growth—mental, emotional, physical, social, financial, and spiritual. Every area is significant and worthy of development. None stands alone. Dr. Hill clearly discusses this in his later books such as *Grow Rich with Peace of Mind* and *You Can Work Your Own Miracles*.

A recent publication of the Napoleon Hill Foundation entitled *Beyond Positive Thinking* is now available. It is a wonderful book that encourages a person not only to think positively, but to act positively as well. Without positive actions, little success occurs. Our formula—Thought + Action = Success—is the overall idea. This book will help you become your very best public relations tool by promoting yourself first.

As you promote yourself to a better position in life, always model your best behavior for others. Show up, work hard, speak success, and wait for the positive effects. These effects will come sooner than you think, and in far greater proportions than you can ever imagine.

<u>REFLECTION</u>

Start by doing what's necessary, then what's possible and suddenly you are doing the impossible.

–FRANCIS OF ASSISI

Lesson 45

You are master of your destiny. You can influence, direct and control your own environment. You can make your life what you want it to be.
—NAPOLEON HILL

In today's competitive world, securing the job of your dreams takes time, talent, and energy. During the interviewing process it is important that you never promise more than you can deliver. However, this being said, you should always be more than willing to go the extra mile for an employer in the area of his or her interests. Too often people mistake going the extra mile in their personal area of interest as if their desire was the same as the employer's immediate need. Don't make this mistake. By doing something that your employer needs to have done, you are building your case for promotion as well as servicing the very real need of the individual who can further your interests when the time comes.

Dr. Hill reminds us to mentally put ourselves in the position of the job that we want to have, and in a period of time physically we will be there too. This reminds me of a story related to those of us who spend some of our free time reading in an area of personal interest. It has been stated that if you read in an area of your interest for thirty minutes a day, within three years you will be known in your community. Add another two years to make five years all the while reading thirty minutes per day in the same area of interest, and you will be known nationally. Finally, add just two more years to total seven, and by reading just thirty minutes a day in this same area, you will be known internationally in this specialized field. Why is this so? First of all, 98% of individuals do not have the self-discipline to read just thirty minutes a day and even more so, 98% of the people cannot stick with or determine a definite area of interest that they want to hitch their star to for peak performance.

Why not thank the Creator for your ability to read, to learn, and to promote yourself into the position of your dreams? The saying goes "nothing ventured, nothing gained." Don't be afraid to stand out from the crowd by having the courage of your convictions. "Say what you mean, and mean what you say" is another often heard admonition. Stand up and make a personalized statement regarding who you are and where you want to be. You've been told that you have to risk climbing out on a limb because that's where the fruit is! It's as simple as deciding what your favorite fruit is, locating it, and then reaching up for the finest apple, peach, plum, cherry, or whatever it is that you want to select for yourself.

Bing Crosby reminds you that when you hitch your wagon to a star you CAN carry moonbeams home in a jar—and be BETTER off than you are! Today as you relax during your Thanksgiving holiday, ask yourself what moonbeams you will be gathering for yourself. And, then, do just that! Remember too, to give thanks and next to be of service. These two things are the "magical ingredients" that work in your behalf every single time that you use them.

REFLECTION
To achieve what you want, you must want enough to achieve.
–WALTER M. GERMAIN

Lesson 46

Taking possession of your positive self will put you on the success beam that you may ride triumphantly to whatever heights of achievement you desire.

—NAPOLEON HILL

Every holiday season I like to see a production of *A Christmas Carol*. This classic work by Charles Dickens transforms and renews our spirit if we are open to the change. The main character, Scrooge, is the extreme manifestation of a negative personality acquired over a lifetime. Inherently, he is not evil but rather a collection of his own worse habits. At the beginning of the story, Scrooge has spiraled down to become an abysmal creature. He hates people, life, and in general all the goodness the yuletide season has to offer. Nothing pleases him. He hits rock bottom when the three ghosts of Christmas Past, Christmas Present, and Christmas Yet to Come force him to take a hard look at his life. Scrooge's transformation occurs when he realizes that all along life was a choice, and he habitually chose to see the negative side of life rather than the positive side. In the musical version of this tale, he states: "I will take the time that I have left to live and I'll give it all I've got to give." This single affirmative statement becomes his definite major purpose and within the wink of an eye you can witness Scrooge's remarkable transformation. It reminds me of the Biblical verse, "Behold I make all things new."

Renewing our lives takes work. Knowing where we are going takes guidance and determination. If we view the 17 principles of success as a roadmap to a positive destiny, we can begin to chart our course one principle at a time. Pleasing Personality is a principle that most people understand, but few practice. A person with a pleasing personality coupled with education and professional training can usually name his salary. Charles Schwab who worked for Andrew Carnegie and often received bonuses of over $1 million per year exemplified this trait. He could work with people because he liked people and understood those who were simple laborers as well as those who ran the company. Carnegie capitalized on Schwab's ability to get along with people, and in doing so furthered his own corporate interests.

Napoleon Hill spoke frequently about the little things such as courtesy, tact, tone of voice, a firm handshake, a welcoming smile, and a positive mental attitude. He believed that when combined with the other 16 principles, that the principle of a pleasing personality could make or break an individual.

Why not start polishing your personality. Try putting a little courtesy into practice. Make a concerted effort to be courteous to every single person whom you meet. Do this for a week, and when you feel that you can be courteous from habit, add another trait for week number two. If you do this consciously for a little over 30 weeks, you will have mastered the traits that Dr. Hill has researched that lead to a pleasing personality. No need to wait for a visit from three ghosts to set your sails on the right course. Do it now, because it is worth doing and it will begin the transformation of your life just as it did so many Christmases past for the life of Ebenezer Scrooge.

REFLECTION
*It is better to correct your own faults
than those of another.*
—DEMOCRITUS

Lesson 47

Only if you have an open mind can you grasp the full impact of the first rule of the Science of Success: Whatever the mind can conceive and believe, the mind can achieve.

—NAPOLEON HILL

The visual and mental imagery that Dr. Hill uses reminds me of the Matrix movies. Challenging us to free our minds and to be open to new ideas takes on great relevance as everywhere we turn people seem to be more intolerant than ever. Through tolerance people learn to live in community even if their beliefs systems are different. Never should it be expected that everyone follow a systematic pattern of uniform beliefs, however, it is asked of us that at least we remain open to new ideas. Without fresh new ideas personal change is thwarted and we stagnate. More of the same does little to bring individuals to a higher level of thinking and living.

Rather than being fearful of change, we need to experience change that is furthered by growth and development. The saying "when you're green you grow, when you're ripe you rot" is as true today as it was yesterday and it will still be true tomorrow. Growth indicates life and is the force that propels us to higher levels. Stagnation precedes death and dying.

Elisabeth Kublër-Ross spent her life researching the death and dying process. She concluded that there were five stages involved in this transition from life to death. They are:

Denial and isolation: "This is not happening to me."

Anger: "How dare God do this to me?"

Bargaining: "Just let me live to see my son graduate."

Depression: "I can't bear to face going through this, putting my family through this."

Acceptance: "I'm ready. I don't want to struggle anymore."

As the stages are analyzed, they appear to be the same steps that individuals go through whenever they are engaged in a change process. Test this on yourself. Consider any major change that you have experienced within the last five years. Ask yourself whether or not you transitioned through the above steps before the change was complete. I am certain for the most part you would have to answer "yes."

Now—for the good news. Since people resist change and are reluctant to make new beginnings, it is beneficial to know that everyone shares similar feelings. Also, whether the change is selected by you for your advancement or forced upon you, it is good to know that the stages of this process are identical for everyone. You might say: "Whew! I am in the depression stage of change, and that is good to know. Now I only have one more step and the change is complete!" Just knowing that a positive end is in sight, makes the entire process more palatable.

Developing an open mind decreases our stress because we no longer have to be the watchdog for the universe. It is not our turn to be on sentry duty! An open mind relaxes our barriers, and creates more harmony and less discord. Just knowing that sometimes human beings do come with a service manual makes the entire process easier to experience. Remember too that Dr. Hill wrote the epitome of the service manual for our success maintenance. It's called the *PMA Science of Success Course* and is available for purchase as either the home study or the distance learning course through the Napoleon Hill

Foundation. With Christmas around the corner, it would make the perfect gift for that person who wants to better his or her life and the lives of others around them!

<u>REFLECTION</u>

We are handicapped by what we think
we can't do.

–MARK TWAIN

Short Lessons on Life
by Napoleon Hill

*Before any alliance of men can constitute a
Master Mind every man in the group must
have his heart as well as his head in full
sympathy with the object of the alliance,
and he must be in perfect harmony with the
leader and every other member of the
alliance.*

*Through some strange form of mind
chemistry with which science is not
familiar, those who literally live by the
Golden Rule, and know why they live by it,
thereby create the mental attitude so
essential to attract the desirable things of
life.*

Lesson 48

> *Change your mental attitude and the world*
> *around you will change accordingly.*
> —NAPOLEON HILL

As Christmas closes in upon us, the "busyness" of the season can cause us to short circuit and burn out just like the lights on our Christmas decorations. When this happens, the usual response is to go into high gear and create more hurry in order to catch up on the things that are remaining undone. Everyone knows that there are gifts to buy, cards to send, wrapping to accomplish, dinners to prepare, and holiday emails to answer. All this time spent in doing the necessary things prevents us from enjoying the spontaneity of a beautiful moment or moments that could become our "forever" or mental screensaver snapshots in time. As chaos escalates, peace and joy recede further and further from our day.

I was on vacation last week, and during that time I decided that I was going to mentally capture a daily snapshot of an inconsequential action—by the world's standards—that contributed to my personal peace and contentment. I promised myself that I would write it down and preserve the memory so that at this time next year I could count 365 actions that made my world a better place in which to live. Let me tell you what prompted this thought.

While on a seven hour bus trip outside of Ixtapa, Mexico we traveled to several locations. One was a small village where we visited a bakery and also had lunch in a nearby town square.

All the ambience of a joyful Mexican holiday season was present—strolling Mariachis, colorful vendors selling local handicrafts, a flavorful slightly alcoholic punch made from pomegranates, and bright green limones accompanying the guacamole and tortilla chips that came to our table. After eating, we strolled through the church and observed the decorations in honor of the feast day, December 12, of Our Lady of Guadalupe. Back on the bus, we settled in for the long ride back.

While observing the sights of the village, the bus driver pointed out a man walking along the sidewalk who he said was 108! His skin was leathered, his head bent, his gait slow, but he was purposeful in his mission. I questioned whether or not he was 108, but nevertheless he was elderly and still pursuing an active life. I mentally wished the same for everyone I knew and held dear.

The bus continued to move down the street slowly, and it was then that I spotted an older girl—maybe 5th or 6th grade—sitting on the curb with a younger boy, perhaps her brother, with her arm around him. School was letting out, and she probably was escorting him home when they stopped a moment to wonder at the busload of tourists who were visiting their hometown. Looking up at the bus, they began to wave and the little boy was busily greeting everyone with his "wave" gesture. Just at that moment, it was my turn to pass by them. I waved, he waved back, and then our eyes aligned. I smiled, he smiled, and then he spontaneously blew me a kiss! What a moment for international relations! Because of its sincerity and uncalculated nature, the little boy's action was entirely heartfelt and engaging. It was one of the highlights of my trip. He asked for nothing, expected nothing, but was just acknowledging my presence and humanity. The United Nations itself could not have done anything more as a gesture of peace and goodwill between nations!

This little boy's actions touched me and the kiss that he threw is my first personal screensaver for world peace! As Gandhi said, "Be the change you want to see in the world." I'm certain that this little Mexican boy did not hear or read this quote, but he had internalized its essence all by himself. He was a living, breathing metaphor for peace and the most priceless souvenir of my trip!

I hope during this holiday season that each of us can find a moment or initiate an action that will touch the heart of another person in the same manner that this little boy's loving action touched me! It was a priceless treasure of my Mexican vacation. What priceless treasures can you give to someone today?

REFLECTION
Don't judge each day by the harvest you
reap, but by the seeds you plant.
–ROBERT LOUIS STEVENSON

SHORT LESSONS ON LIFE
by Napoleon Hill

*The educated man is the man who has
learned how to get everything he needs
without violating the rights of his fellow
men. Education comes from within; you get
it by struggle and effort and thought.*

*The successful man makes it his business to
read books, and to learn important facts
concerning his chosen work which have
come from the experience of other men who
have gone before him.*

Lesson 49

*Faith without action is dead. It is the art
of believing by doing, coming as a result
of persistent action.*

—NAPOLEON HILL

Christmas will be here in just a few days, and the rush is on to get all the last minute things done before Santa arrives. Spirits are high and a feeling of belief is in the air. Children believe in the magic of the season and adults believe in goodwill and peace. Unfortunately, as Dr. Hill reminds us, people use the word belief and wish interchangeably today. These words do not mean the same thing or hold the same power. For example, just wishing someone a Merry Christmas and a Happy New Year doesn't guarantee that things will happen to make their holiday merry any more than wishing on a distant star. Belief, on the other hand, is rock solid and when spoken and emotionalized with enthusiasm whatever is believed comes to pass and can be witnessed, verified, and documented.

Our emotions strengthen our beliefs and give them fuel for manifestation. Wishes, on the other hand, are light and airy and lacking in substance. Like all fantasies, they evaporate in the light of reality. Belief shines like the sun and cannot be eradicated. Beliefs are beyond ideas, opinions, attitudes, and values. They are the substance of things unheard of and yet unseen, but more real than the houses we live in or the cars we drive. Beliefs are our cornerstone of reality and the foundation of who we are.

Why not capitalize on helping someone believe in themselves this holiday season? Tell a child that you believe in him and in what he is capable of becoming. Tell a co-worker that you believe that she can outshine last year's performance. Tell a minister that you believe in his message and that his Sunday sermon grabbed your heart. Tell an unemployed person that you believe his skills will secure him a job this month. Now, do one more thing. Back your belief in the person with action. Help the child research jobs that he may have the talent to pursue. Help the co-worker list things that she has accomplished that have been noteworthy and plan for more of the same. Help the minister get his message out to more people by bringing friends to the service. And, help the unemployed man pursue job leads by scheduling a time to look together for employment opportunities. Your thought plus action will equal success for the person you lend a helping hand to. And, more importantly, that person will never forget it.

Here is a personal note that I received from a friend today with a Christmas gift. I believe the note will exist forever—at least in my memory. It reads:

> *I want to thank you for all the times you have encouraged me and even given me that 'little' push to go further. I am truly blessed in all the things you have done for me. I can't explain in words how grateful I am. Thank you for your friendship and may I bless you the same in the coming years!*

Wow! What a feel good Christmas present. Not only am I storing up the positive karma, but now I want to go out and do more good! This is the spirit of Christmas that I believe in—and I hope that you experience that belief this season too!

REFLECTION
Happiness is as a butterfly, which, when pursued, is always beyond our grasp, but which, if you will sit down quietly, may alight upon you.
–NATHANIEL HAWTHORNE

Lesson 50

*You must believe that what you want will
happen, and you must take the necessary
action to ensure it.*

—NAPOLEON HILL

As the clock ticks down the old year and we await the arrival of a brand new year, most people begin to wonder what will occur during the next twelve months. If we have a wait and see attitude, then whatever happens simply happens. However, if we want to be a co-creator of our own universe we must make plans with a purpose in order to manifest the destiny that we foresee for ourselves. Some people say that we cannot control the future, but failing to plan is planning to fail. Like everyone else, I like to forecast things that I desire for the new year, but I also know that unless I put determined, concentrated effort behind my goals they will never materialize. We have to distinguish between a wish and a desire. Dr. Hill even goes so far as to say we must have a burning desire. In a comparative manner, a wish could be a spark, a desire a flame, and a burning desire a bonfire—see the difference?

Our year is divided into 12 months, so why not assign yourself 12 goals for the new year? If you want to, you can even rank the goals highest to lowest with one being your number one goal for the year. Once you have penned this list, look at it morning, noon, and night. Expose the list to your subconscious mind through repetition, and soon enough the recitation of the list will become a habit, and you will just say it automatically like the ABC's or the multiplication tables. That's when your subconscious mind is assigned the task of making your goals materialize for you. Dr. Hill tells us that when this happens your subconscious mind will deliver a plan to you that will be the turnkey in achieving your goals. He goes on to add that we should not question the plan, but act on it at once because the moment of inspiration may pass, your enthusiasm may wane, and then you are back to the beginning stage—the wish stage—of making things happen.

Don't wish—believe—and then you will make it so.

May this be your most creative New Year ever! I believe in you.

REFLECTION
I avoid looking forward or backward, and
try to keep looking upward.
—CHARLOTTE BRONTE

Lesson 51

Clearly define to yourself what you want to attain in life. Say to yourself: I can do it. I can do it now. Make a plan and chart the steps you must take to reach your goal. Take them one at a time, and you will find that with each success the next step comes easier and easier as more and more people are attracted to help you achieve your ultimate purpose.

—NAPOLEON HILL

Over the years, many poems or segments of poems have appeared in works by Dr. Hill and W. Clement Stone. One that parallels the thought expressed in the Golden Rule commentary is an anonymous poem that is entitled *Today*.

TODAY

I shall do so much in the years to come,
But what have I done today?
I shall give out gold in princely sum,
But what did I give today?
I shall lift the heart and dry the tear
I shall plant a hope in the place of fear
I shall speak with words of love and cheer,
But what have I done today?
I shall bring to each lonely life a smile
But give to truth a greater birth
And to steadfast faith a deeper worth,
I shall feed the hungering souls of earth,
But whom have I fed today?

As each of us considers the actions that we are taking today and their consequences, I strongly encourage you to review the outcomes that are occurring in your life. The level of respect that we have for the areas in our life essentially determines what type of life we have. Ask yourself, are you respectful of your family, friends, finances, appearance, education, work, and home? Your answer will determine your actions, and your actions will determine your outcome. For example, if you want more friendships in your life, take action and be more of a friend to others yourself. If you want more money in your life, ask yourself how respectful are you of the income you have now? In order to create more of whatever you desire, you must acknowledge with respect what you already have, and then take purposeful action in order to make it more so.

As you write and review your resolutions, plan to take action on what it is you want to increase in your life and likewise plan to ignore what it is you want to decrease in your life. You always get what you focus on. Focus on the good, and good will surely come to you.

REFLECTION
Chances are right now you are standing in the middle of your own acre of diamonds.
–EARL NIGHTINGALE

Lesson 52

Every adversity you meet carries with it a seed of equivalent or greater benefit. Realize this statement, and believe in it. Close the door of your mind on all the failures and circumstances of your past so your mind can operate in a Positive Mental Attitude. Every problem has a solution—you only have to find it!

—NAPOLEON HILL

Are you able to articulate your success plan? Can you state it, write it out, and sign and date it? Can you recall it at will? Do you know the steps to its completion? Is the master plan of your life first and foremost in your mind's eye, or is it an afterthought? How does one chart one's course, set sail, stay the course and arrive in port on schedule?

In Napoleon Hill's **Road Map to Success**, he details the sequential steps to success one by one. Although the outline is easily understood, most people cannot achieve the success they wish for in life because they do not have the personal initiative, self-discipline, and persistence that is required to meet their goal. People who fail in their pursuit of their definite major purpose are not capable of aligning themselves to their self-determined burning desire and sticking like barnacles to it until completion—often under "insur-mountable" odds.

Each of us has "insurmountable" odds. Those of us who acknowledge these odds have already succumbed to them. The old tapes that are repeated again and again in our mind that state—I'm too old; I'm not qualified; I have no means of support; I do not have the right friends; I cannot succeed when everyone else in my family has failed, etc., all ring true right on schedule—just as we predicted that they would. You've heard of the self-fulfilling prophecy, right?

What's a person to do? Well, if you are sincere in your journey you must overcome the obstacles just like Odysseus did when he refused to succumb to the Sirens' song. He refused to be controlled by forces outside of himself, and he would not allow himself to be dashed on the rocks of personal failure. He stood firm in his determination to complete his journey and to arrive home.

Ask yourself who or what are your Sirens? Are they habits that you have permitted to invade your life and to control your destiny? Perhaps you can readily point a finger at your Achilles' heel, or perhaps you cannot. But, I guarantee you that if you are not reaching for success in a systematic, planned manner, you will never arrive at your goal. Read about Odysseus and his journey. Read about Achilles and his vulnerable heel. Read stories that outline a hero's journey. Then, become the star in your own life's work. See the obstacles as challenges that prove your worth. When the journey becomes a game with you winning the coveted prize, you will have captured the idea of what it takes to achieve. See yourself succeeding and you will be the success you continually envision in your life right on schedule. Can you see it?

REFLECTION
The purpose of life, after all, is to live it, to taste experience to the utmost, to reach out eagerly and without fear for newer and richer experience.
—ELEANOR ROOSEVELT

AS THE YEAR BEGINS ANEW . . . HAVE FAITH IN YOU!

*A Positive Mental Attitude . . . PMA. . . is a
can-do and will-try attitude. It is the right, honest,
constructive thought action or reaction
to any person, situation or set of circumstances.
It can be developed through self-discipline and
willpower. Keep saying "I can. . .I will."
A Positive Mental Attitude is the catalyst
for achieving worthwhile success.*

–NAPOLEON HILL

How do we identify faith? When giving advice many people simple say to have faith and everything will turn out okay. What is this elusive faith that so many individuals seem connected to as if they had a land line to Infinite Intelligence and others of us always get a busy signal or even worse get disconnected? "Try your call again later," "all lines are busy," and "leave a message and someone will get back to you" seem to be the persistent responses for those who are not linked in to the faith network.

Norman Vincent Peale states that you should "Believe in yourself! Have faith in your abilities! Without a humble but reasonable confidence in your own powers you cannot be successful or happy." Paracelsus, a writer of ancient wisdom, adds: "whether the object of your faith be real or false, you will nevertheless obtain the same effects." Those who get results from faith tell us that we cannot be objective about it. Rather, we must be subjective. Your belief must be firmly implanted at the subconscious level for it to make a profound impact in your life. It is never too late to begin to develop faith. Here are some key steps in the development of faith that will speed up your call.

1. According to Dr. Hill, applied faith is the only faith that works. You must do in order to receive. Just thinking and anticipating is not enough. Faith is action.

2. Faith works in your life when you believe in yourself. You must have self-confidence in your talents and capabilities. Consider your assets, bolster your self-esteem, engage your personal power, and then act.

3. Act as if you knew the final outcome already, and it is the positive one you are expecting. Emerson states: "Do the thing and you will have the power."

4. Biblically, we are told "faith without works is dead." You must plan and work for the results you want. Faith needs to work in tandem with action, not independent of it.

5. Emotionalize your faith. When emotion is attached to a goal, this burning desire proceeds to materialize faster than an ordinary desire does without it. Make sure that your emotions are positive and your results will be positive as well.

6. Affirmations—auto-suggestions—assist you in moving from objective faith to subjective faith. If you want different results, you must change the software, so you can run a new program.

7. It is never too late to be the success you envision for yourself. It takes the principle of applied faith to kick you into the success mode. See something good for yourself, and in the words of Captain Picard, "Make it so." Be what you might have been before somebody else beats you to it.

8. Simply, do the thing, and you will have the power.

9. Bertolt Brecht states: "You can make a fresh start with your final breath." And, Dr. Hill writes that "It's never too late."

10. By acting with subjective faith you will accomplish what you desire most in life. The key is subjective belief followed by action.

<u>REFLECTION</u>

It is not light that we need but fire; it is not the gentle shower, but thunder. We need the storm, the whirlwind, and the earthquake.

–FREDERICK DOUGLASS

For additional information about Napoleon Hill products please contact the following location:

Napoleon Hill Foundation
University of Virginia-Wise
College Relations Apt. C
1 College Avenue
Wise, VA 24293

Don Green, Executive Director
Annedia Sturgill, Executive Assistant

Telephone: 276-328-6700
email: napoleonhill@uvawise.edu

Website: www.naphill.org